WELCOME TO THE NEW YEAR'S ENERGIES OF WATER TIGER 2022

The past year may have been incredibly challenging for you. Many countries have had to adapt to different ways of keeping their people safe and protected from the pandemic that has brought so much chaos to the world.

It is true to say that the world has been turned upside down with COVID-19!

The last year has been a genuine test of human spirit and one's strength of self.

We have all had to adjust our lifestyles to the new reality, adapting to different severities of lockdown, in different ways. How we adapted depended on where we lived, government policies, family dynamics how one was confined and the ability to revitalize and nourish one selves.

Can in this new reality, Feng Shui help?

Feng shui has no magic cure, however knowledge and placement using symbolic cures may help reduce vulnerability to current times.

2022 is the Year of Water Tiger. The coming year is dominated by this dynamic and charming creature. The Tiger - because of the sheer, raw power of the Tiger, is honored in China as the ultimate protector of home, family and health. The Tiger's warm hearted, sociable, and friendly. The year 2022 brings the lucky Tiger, which represents the greatest power on earth and is the emblem of protection for human life.

2022 Astrology & Feng Shui diary gives you the advantage of being prepared with daily insight into your health, harmony, love, and business opportunities. Providing you with tips for your home from Chinese Astrology, Flying Star and the school of Bagua.

Tune into the changes and energies you need to take into consideration during 2022.

- 2022 brings forth a year of action and change.
- A Time for Optimism and Empathy!
- A period of movement and will.
- Unforeseen changes and surprising developments
- A year for transparency, communication, calm, balance and moderation.
- The Water TIGER is synonymous with kindness, alertness, curiosity, intelligence.
- The Water Tiger can be rash, impulsive, dynamic and full of energy.
- The Water TIGER promotes justice, morality and strong leadership.
- 2022 TIGER possess a great sense of morals, is calm, fair and just, confident and self-assured.

Understanding and applying the wonderful science of Feng Shui helps to better adapt to the changing times and energies within our environment, home, country and world . There is always a need to adjust to the dynamic nature of the winds that blow and the waters that flow. Feng Shui literally means "wind and water". Wind is the energy of our breath and water represents how we choose to exist in the flow of life...

May 2022 bring you health harmony and prosperity.

COMPLETE FENG SHUI DIARY 2022 – YEAR OF WATER TIGER

Published by Complete Feng Shui

Mb: 0421 116 799,

Email: michele@completefengshui.com

Websites: www.completefengshui.com

Complete Feng Shui Diary 2022 ©

Text copyright © Michele Castle Illustrations copyright © Michele Castle / Lucy Deslandes

All rights reserved, no part of this publication may be reproduced, stored in a retrieval system or transmitted, in any form, or by any means, electronic, mechanical, photocopying, recording, or otherwise, without the prior written permission from Complete Feng Shui.

The moral right of the author to be identified as the author of this book has been asserted.

Author: Michele Castle

Design copyright @completefengshui

Title: Complete Feng Shui Diary 2022 - Year of Water Tiger

ISBN: 978-0-6452137-4-4

January 2022

This Planner has been written to offer insight and planning for daily activities and energies of 2022 from Flying Stars, Bagua, Chinese astrology, and date selection. The author editor and publisher take no responsibility for the outcome of any information implemented from this planner.

Platinum member of the Association of Feng Shui Consultants (AFSC)

Recognised Feng Shui training institution by the (AFSC)

 facebook@completefengshui    instagram@completefengshui

Compatible Chinese Animals Sign in 2022:
Horse, Dog and Pig

Incompatible Chinese animals in 2022:
Monkey and Snake

Good Travel Directions in 2022:
Southeast, Northwest, North and Northeast

Lucky colours for 2022:
White, Gold, Silver, Blue, and green

YOUR PERSONAL INFORMATION

Name..

Date of Birth...

Time of Birth..

Animal Sign..

Address...

....

....

Telephone No..Office No. ....

Mobile No..Fax No. ....

E-mail address...

Favorite Websites...

....

Secret Friend...Allies ....

Conflict Animal..

Peach Blossom Animal..

Self-Element..

Kua Number...

Your House Facing Direction...

Office Direction...

Best Direction (Sheng Chi)..Health Direction (Tien Yi) ....

Romance Direction (Nien Yen)..................................Personal Growth Direction (Fu Wei) ....

Unlucky (Ho Hai)..Five Ghost (Wu Kwei) ....

Six Killings (Lui Sha)..Total Loss (Chueh Ming) ....

RESOLUTIONS FOR 2022

In Chinese culture, Tigers are guardians. Tiger energy is believed to guard against fire, theft and spirits because of the sheer dynamic raw power of the Tiger. The Tiger is honored in China as the ultimate protector. The Tiger represents the greatest power on earth and is the emblem of protection for human life.

CONTENTS

Personal details	7
Resolutions for 2022	9
How to Use the Complete Feng Shui diary	13
The Chinese Astrology wheel & the 12 animal signs	14
Understanding Chinese Astrology Animals	15
Secret friends, Astrological Allies & Conflict Animals	17
Location of the Tai Sui in different years	18
2022 Afflictions	20
Flying Star Feng Shui	22
Favourable Stars / Unfavourable Stars	23
Kua numbers	25
Auspicious and Inauspicious directions based on your Kua number	30
Your personal Kua Directions	31
The Four Celestial Guardians	32
Special Animal Pairings	33
January Ox	36
January Flying Stars	38
February Tiger	44
February Flying Stars	46
March Rabbit	52
March Flying Stars	54
Activating Feng Shui in the Garden	58
April Dragon	62
April Flying Stars	64
May Snake	70
May Flying Stars	72
June Horse	78
June Flying Stars	80
July Goat	86
July Flying Stars	88
August Monkey	96
August Flying Stars	98
September Rooster	104
September Flying Stars	106
Activating peach blossom luck for love	110
October Dog	114
October Flying Stars	116
November Pig	122
November Flying Stars	124
December Rat	130
December Flying Stars	132
Good and bad days based on animal signs	136
Calendar 2023	138
Transform Your Life Feng Shui Retreat experience	142
About author	145
Testimonials	146

HOW TO USE THE COMPLETE FENG SHUI DIARY

Clarity and good timing are vital in ensuring whatever you undertake is given the best possible chance of success. Even simple everyday activities can lead to huge negative outcomes if they are riddled with obstacles and bad energy.

ACTIVITY ICONS
This diary contains specially calculated auspicious dates for significant activities like travelling, moving, renovating, having a haircut or signing a contract. These are marked by icons on each page.

 Travelling   Moving    Renovating    Haircut    Signing Contract

Understanding The Icons
FAVOURABLE DAYS FOR SPECIFIC TASKS
The icons on each page reveal favourable days for travelling, love and relationship luck, harmonious days, making friends, moving house, signing contracts, having a haircut, starting construction and renovating.

 Travelling   Love and relationship luck   Harmonious day   To meeting friends   Moving

 Signing Contarct    Haircut   Renovating

Unfavorable days are also indicated for poor health with low life force energy and major activities on clash days.

 Health    Major activity's day of clash

Use the waxing cycle of the moon for initiating new projects and the waning cycle for terminating activities.

THE LUNAR CYCLE
Taking note of the lunar cycle enables with choosing the best date for activities. The period between the new and full moon is known as the waxing cycle and is a favourable time for undertaking activities which need growth energy i.e., starting a new project, new journey, opening a new business or signing a deal. The waning cycle (between full moon and new moon) is a good period to shut down something as this is a period when the moon's energy is declining, i.e., closing your business, putting things into storage, finalising a divorce, ending a relationship, starting a diet, quitting smoking, are all good activities during this period.

HOW TO USE THE COMPLETE FENG SHUI DIARY

CHINESE ASTROLOGY ANIMALS
Included in each day's summary are good/bad days for certain animal signs. When undertaking any significant activity, always check whether it is a good/bad day for your sign, as this overrides whatever is indicated by the icons. e.g., if it is a bad day for the Tiger, then all activities will NOT be auspicious for the Tiger that day, no matter what the icons indicate. The Tiger must avoid scheduling important matters that day.

Each of the twelve astrological animals occupies 15 degrees of the compass. Your astrological direction always brings you good luck.

UNDERSTANDING CHINESE ASTROLOGY ANIMALS

The 12 Chinese astrological animals are all quite different and unique in their own way.

Rat	**Rabbit**	**Horse**	**Rooster**
Ox/Bull	**Dragon**	**Goat/Sheep**	**Dog**
Tiger	**Snake**	**Monkey**	**Pig/Boar**

Rat: Enduring, persistent, adaptable, accepting, brave, curious and forgiving. Can talk too freely and can be accused of gossiping. They are fast, determined, they don't stay put and have many changes and moves in all areas of their lives; they are excited by new things.

Ox: The hardest worker of all the animals; they are persistent, will take the pressure off others, have a high stamina, and will carry heavy burdens. They can be stubborn, reveal very little including their health and they seldom complain. They also tend to stay put for extended periods of time.

Tiger: Sensitive, alert, has a lot of energy, influential and some can be bad tempered. They are usually leaders, take chances and lead fortunate lives. They are also independent and very protective of their family and friends.

Rabbit: Exceptionally sensitive, alert, intelligent and honest. Their minds move at great speeds, they are clever, analytical and will always have back-up plans. They are soft, emotional, sensitive and quick tempered, but very rarely express it. They can be impatient, vulnerable and believe it or not, they are a great asset to have.

Dragon: Spirit of great power, wisdom, strength and energy. They can look down on people, but they work and accomplish on grand scale. Love a challenge, gains respect and support of others. They are dreamers, creative, optimistic, steady and firm. Dragons are generally very good in business.

Snake: Sensitive, very perceptive, alert and enjoys life to the full. Goal orientated, persistent, alert, loyal, patient, but unforgiving. They make great friends – do *not* make them your enemy. Snakes tend to acquire knowledge and then move on. They are determined and can be wise.

Horse: Devoted, inner-strength, persistent, hard-working and determined. They are dependable, honest, loyal and love challenges. They are proud and independent, but they need companions. Horse's also like the comforts of life. They can be frivolous and love to gossip.

Goat: Stable, determined, hard-working and willing. They are survivors. They make wonderful team workers, not leaders. They are observant, great listeners and need to have people around them. Goats like harmony, but don't like to be alone.

Monkey: Fast thinkers, very quick learners, creative, but can be insensitive. They don't bear grudges, are highly independent and make friends quickly. They are helpful, self-confident, high achievers, ambitious, competitive, determined and very rarely give up.

Rooster: Unique energy in relationships and friendships. They are musical, creative, artistic, imaginative and inventive; can be drama Queens or Kings. They can be focused and when it is something they want they will love it with a passion. They are persistent, know what they want, are great talkers and they are great debaters and negotiators. They are straight forward, honest with others and make great friends. They are sensitive to relationships, vulnerable and they tend to bottle up their feelings. They will rarely fight back, but when they do it is with full power.

Dog: Ready for action, energetic, gains respect, brave, but they take risks. They are helpful, loyal, reliable, determined, competent and confident. Dogs will not let go of ideas and ambitions and are likely to see things to the end. They are caring and a great listener. They are very efficient and make great workers, but they are not leaders.

Pig: Energy of wealth in many forms, has a sense of time, but not in a hurry, can be sluggish and not ambitious. Not very intellectually competitive and has natural humility. They accumulate and are usually rotund. They are accepting, intelligent, perceptive, independent and can be considerably determined. They are also reliable and wise in times of a crisis.

Remember, not everyone born in the same year has the same characteristics or personalities. Therefore, the Four Pillars of Destiny Chart gives you a more detailed description of a person born in a year.

SECRET FRIEND, ALLIES AND CONFLICT ANIMALS

ANIMAL SIGN	SECRET FRIEND	ALLIES	CONFLICT ANIMAL
Rat	Ox	Dragon, Monkey	Horse
Ox	Rat	Snake, Rooster	Goat
Tiger	Pig	Horse, Dog	Monkey
Rabbit	Dog	Goat, Pig	Rooster
Dragon	Rooster	Rat, Monkey	Dog
Snake	Monkey	Ox, Rooster	Boar
Horse	Goat	Tiger, Dog	Rat
Sheep	Horse	Rabbit, Pig	Ox
Monkey	Snake	Rat, Dragon	Tiger
Rooster	Dragon	Ox, Snake	Rabbit
Dog	Rabbit	Tiger, Horse	Dragon
Pig	Tiger	Rabbit, Goat	Snake

The Competitors
RAT, MONKEY, DRAGON

These are action-oriented, competitive and determined individuals. The Rat tends to be insecure, requiring Dragon's courage.

The Dragon is headstrong and needs the craftiness of the Monkey and Rat's astute eye for opportunity.

The Monkey is fueled by Dragon's enthusiasm and buoyed by Rat's intelligence.

The Intellectuals
SNAKE, ROOSTER, OX

These are the visionaries of the Zodiac. They are purposeful, resolute and have formidable capabilities, as well as unwavering and strong personalities. The Ox is rock solid but benefits from Snake's charm and Rooster's flamboyance. The Snake is ambitious but will go further If helped by the Ox or Rooster. The Rooster's forthrightness will be tempered by the seductive Snake or the Ox's stable approach.

The Independents
HORSE, DOG, TIGER

These are free spirits; emotional, impetuous and restless. The Horse is the strategist but needs Tiger's impulses to get started and Dog's determination to see things through. The Tiger's ferocity needs to be tempered by Dog's good nature, while the Horse's restless spirit requires an outlet which Tiger provides, or the calming influence which the Dog can give.

The Diplomats
RAT, MONKEY, DRAGON

These are cooperative, low-profile types.

They are sensitive, sympathetic and eager to please. These are not risk takers. The Rabbit's astuteness safeguards Goat's generosity, while the Goat benefits from the Rabbit's sense of priorities. The Pig's strength complements Rabbit's strategic thinking and the Goat's gentler approach.

LOCATION OF THE TAI SUI IN DIFFERENT YEARS

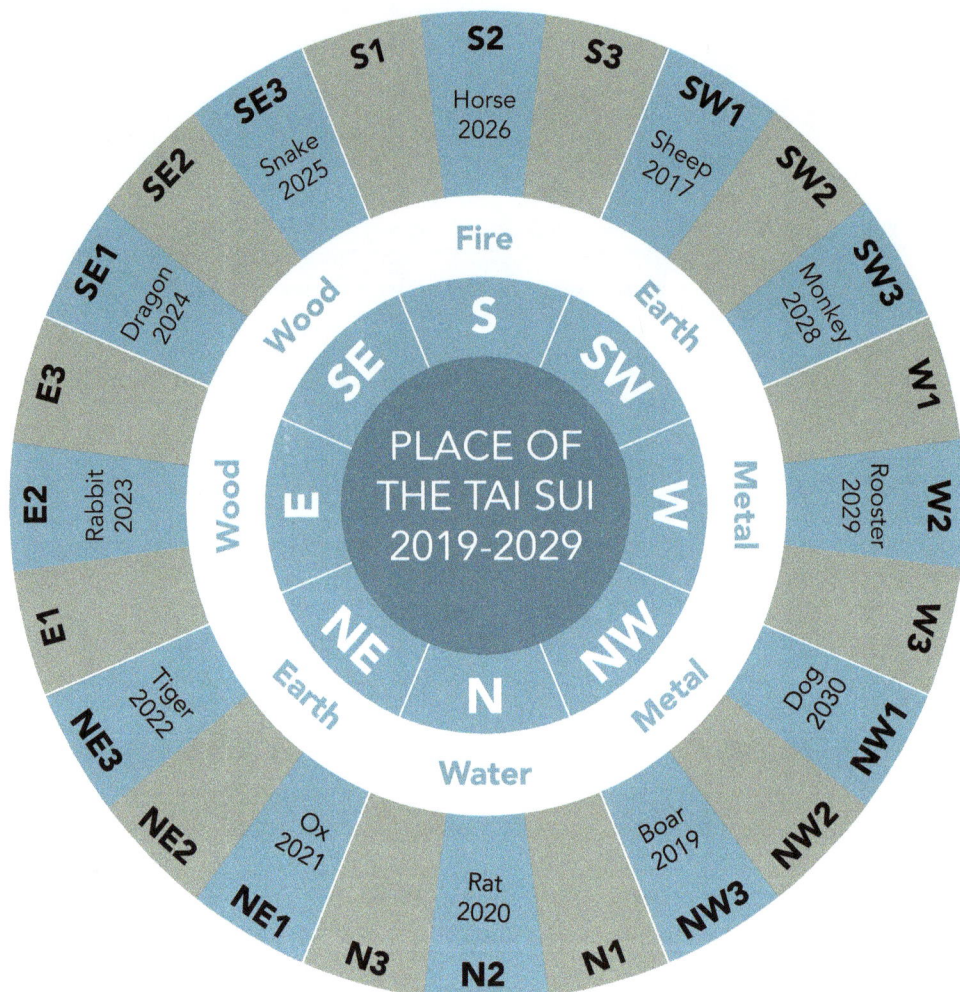

This year 2022

Each year the Tai Sui follows the changing animal sign and moves his residence to the location of the new animal sign. In the Water Tiger Year of 2022, the Tai Sui moves from the Ox direction (Northeast 1) to the direction and location of the Tiger, which is Northeast 3.

Try not to "offend" the Tai Sui by renovating, banging or digging in his location. You must also avoid facing him while dining, studying, working or closing deals. Doing any of this will bring misfortune. The best method of dealing with the Tai Sui is to appease him with a pair of Pi Yao. You should also place the Tai Sui Plaque 2022 in his location of Northeast 3.

2022 AFFLICTIONS

In 2022, the **Northeast** (52.6 – 67.5) is also where the Tai Sui "God of the year" (also known as the Grand Duke) will be located for the year. The Grand Duke is an energy point from the universe that is classed as a God which should always be respected and never disturbed or confronted. It is strongly advised that you *avoid any major renovations or any kind of earthmoving* in this sector for the year and keep this area quiet. You can place a Chi Lin, Pi Yao and Fu Dog in the Northeast 3 facing the Southwest 3 - to appease and assist this sector. But best to not disturb in the first place.

In 2022, The Three Killings, which is an energy force, has also moved to the **North.** When disturbed, The Three Killings tend to bring sickness and health issues, as well as multiple confrontations. You are best to not sit with The Three Killings behind you, instead you should face them.

It is strongly advised that you avoid any major renovations or any kind of earthmoving in this sector for the year and keep this area quiet. You can place strong plant or earth energy of crystals in the **North** to exhaust Three Killings. But best not to disturb or renovate in the first place.

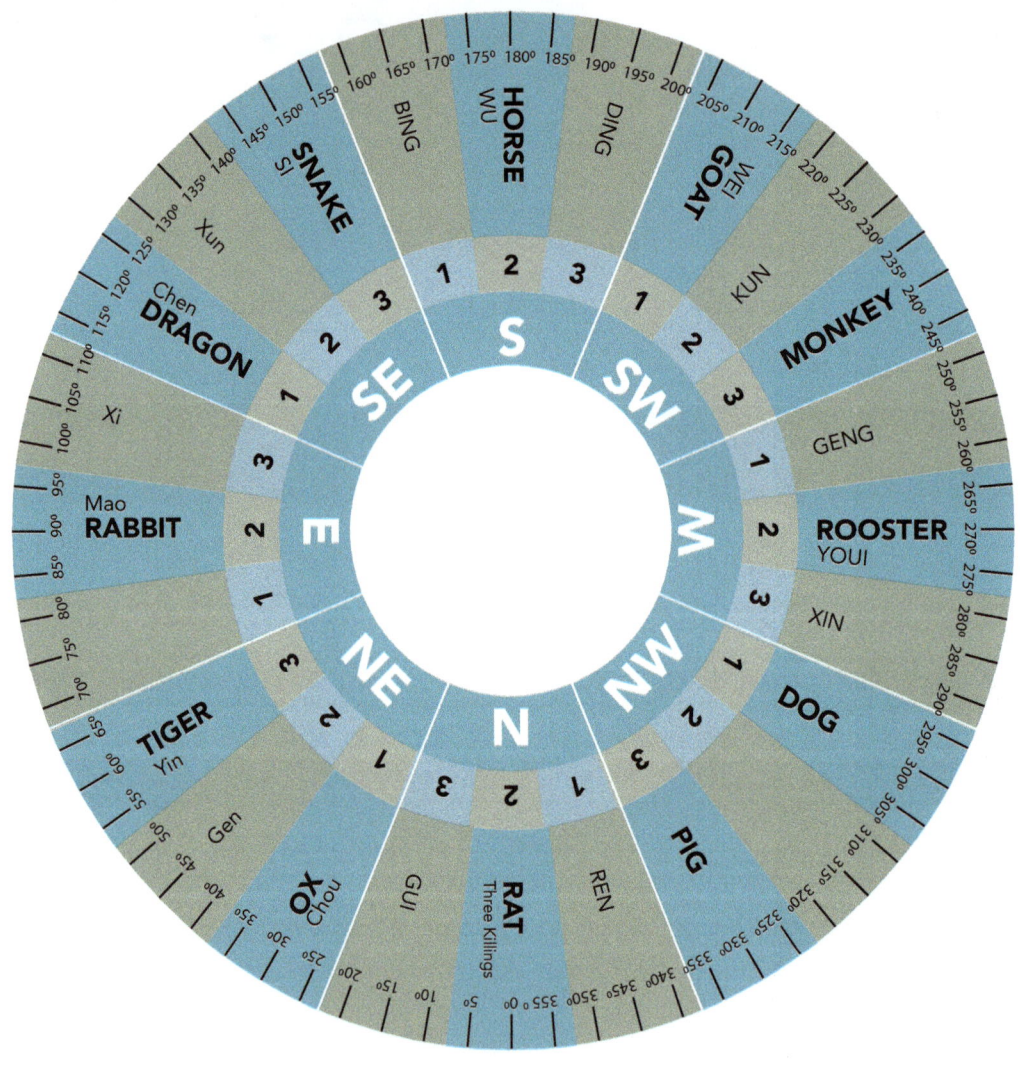

FLYING STAR FENG SHUI

Getting your Feng Shui right for the coming year and energising the auspicious sectors of 2022 will help ensure you have a smooth-sailing and successful year ahead.

As we move from one year to the next, energy changes. Transforming from Yin to Yang, from element to element, from one animal sign to the next. Depending on the ruling element and animal, from one month to the next the energy in the home and its occupant's also changes. Time exerts a very strong impact on your Feng Shui, your luck and destiny.

Good Feng Shui cannot and does not last forever. It must be recharged with small, but significant changes every year. Energy must be refreshed, reorganised and re-energised. Spaces and places need rejuvenating. Energy must be kept moving.

The Flying Stars formula of Feng Shui is a technical approach that directly addresses the effect of time on the energy of homes and businesses and holds a wonderful promise which enables you to improve your luck tremendously. The 2022 Feng Shui chart maps out the distribution of energy in each of the eight sectors of the compass, as well as the center.

The best strategy is always to take care of the negative Stars first, and then concentrate on boosting the good Stars. Pay closer attention to the sectors where your main door, living room and bedrooms are located. The luck present in the main door and living room sector affects everyone in the household, while the bedroom alters the luck of those who sleep in it.

The daily Flying Star number reveals the energy of the day. By understanding the Flying Stars meaning and energy you can determine the quality of luck for each day.

FAVOURABLE STARS

North 1 Victory Triumph and Success Star (**Water Element**): Helps attain victory over competition, enhances career promotion and monetary growth. Strengthen and enhance energy by placement of a Victory Horse, Ruyi, or Dragon Tortoise. A water feature would also be especially beneficial.

Southeast 4 Romance and Literacy Star (**Wood Element**): Good Star which improves relationship opportunities and study and literary fortune for writers and scholars. Enhance luck with bright lights fire energy and wood energy. Place Mandarin Ducks or Huggers, along with peach blossom animals, plants and fresh flowers in this area.

Northwest 6 Heavenly Luck Star (**Metal Element**): Associated with good fortune and help from heaven, brings speculative luck as well as power and authority. Use bright lights, a water feature and Metal to enhance such as Six Gold Coins on red tassel, and Gold Ingots within this area. A Horse will also assist.

Northeast 8 Current Prosperity Star (**Earth Element**): Signifies wealth, prosperity, success and happiness; regarded as the most auspicious Star of all the nine numbers until 2024... Strengthen and enhance by placing any form of wealth symbolism such as a Buddha, Wealth God, Six Gold Coins on red tassel, or Gold Ingots, and a water feature or a picture of water in this area. Activate and use the area as often as possible.

South 9 Multiplying Future Prosperity Star (**Fire Element**): Signifies future prosperity; spurs celebrations, festivities, gatherings and excellent good luck. Enhance the south with bright lights, any wealth symbolism such as a Buddha, a Wealth God, 9 Gold Coins on red tassel, or Gold Ingots.

UNFAVOURABLE STARS

Southwest 2 Sickness Star (**Earth Element**): This illness bringing Star has negative influences on health issues, bringing physical ailments and diseases. . . Supress the energy with placing a Wu Lou (Health Gourd), Six Gold Coins on red tassel, a Saltwater Cure and a Quan Yin in the South West.

East 3 Hostile, Conflict and Dispute Star (**Wood Element**): A bad Star which signifies lawsuits, hostility and quarrels. Brings misunderstandings amongst staff, clients and colleagues, and trouble with the authorities. I recommend placing Fire energy in this area such as bright lights, a red piece of paper, or you can use any red décor object. If your front door is in this area I recommend placing Temple Lions and the Evil Eye symbol. Remove any excess water or plants. Remove Metal windchimes. Do not overstimulate with radio or TV energy.

Centre 5 Misfortune and Obstacles Star (**Earth Element**): Also known as Wu Wang or 5 Yellow Star: It is considered the most malevolent and dangerous of the nine Stars, it brings all kind of misfortunes, accidents, losses and death. Subdue with a Brass 5 element Pagoda, and a Saltwater Cure in the centre. A Ganesha will also assist with removing of obstacles. Keep electrical equipment to a minimum and avoid the colours red and yellow. Try to avoid any major activity within this sector.

West 7 Robbery and Evil Star (**Metal Element**): This unlucky star brings loss, robbery, violence, and gossip to the West sector. Suppress by placing three pieces of Lucky Bamboo in a vase of water, and bright lights in this area, along with the Evil Eye Symbol, and one Blue Rhinoceros and one Blue Elephant, or two Blue Rhinoceroses for extra protection. If your front door is located here, I also recommend Temple Lions.

KUA NUMBERS

A quick way to assess whether a day is lucky for you is to look at the Flying Star number of the day. If the number matches your Kua number, or a number in the same group as your Kua number, then this day is lucky for you. e.g. if the Flying Star number of the day is 6, then the day is auspicious for those whose Kua number is 6, as well as those in West Group (Kua 2, 5, 7 and 8). To determine your personal Kua number, consult tables provided between pages 44-54. Back of diary

YEAR OF BIRTH	ANIMAL SIGN	HEAVENLY STEM	BORN BETWEEN...	MEN	MEN
1900	Rat	Metal	Jan 31, 1900-Feb 18, 1901	1	5
1901	Ox	Metal	Feb 19,1901 - Feb 7, 1902	9	6
1902	Tiger	Water	Feb 8, 1902-Jan 28, 1903	8	7
1903	Rabbit	Water	Jan 29,1903-Feb 28, 1904	7	8
1904	Dragon	Wood	Feb 16,1904- Feb 3,1905	6	9
1905	Snake	Wood	Feb 4, 1905-Jan 24, 1906	5	1
1906	Horse	Fire	Jan 25,1906-Feb 12,1907	4	2
1907	Goat	Fire	Feb 13, 1907- Feb 1, 1908	3	3
1908	Monkey	Earth	Feb 2,1908-Jan 21, 1909	2	4
1909	Rooster	Earth	Jan 22,1909- Feb 9,1910	1	5
1910	Dog	Metal	Feb 10, 1910-Jan 29,1911	9	6
1911	Pig	Metal	Jan 30,1911 - Feb 17,1912	8	7
1912	Rat	Water	Feb 18, 1912-Feb 5, 1913	7	8
1913	Ox	Water	Feb 6, 1913-Jan 25, 1914	6	9
1914	Tiger	Wood	Jan 26,1914- Feb 13, 1915	5	1
1915	Rabbit	Wood	Feb 14,1915-Feb 2,1916	4	2
1916	Dragon	Fire	Feb 3,1916-Jan 22,1917	3	3
1917	Snake	Fire	Jan 23, 1917- Feb 10, 1918	2	4
1918	Horse	Earth	Feb 11,1918-Jan 31, 1919	1	5
1919	Goat	Earth	Feb 1,1919-Feb 19, 1920	9	6
1920	Monkey	Metal	Feb 20, 1920-Feb 7, 1921	8	7
1921	Rooster	Metal	Feb 8,1921 - Jan 27, 1922	7	8
1922	Dog	Water	Jan 28, 1922-Feb 15, 1923	6	9
1923	Pig	Water	Feb 16,1923- Feb 4, 1924	5	1
1924	Rat	Wood	Feb 5, 1924-Jan 23, 1925	4	2
1925	Ox	Wood	Jan 24, 1925- Feb 12, 1926	3	3
1926	Tiger	Fire	Feb 13,1926- Feb 1,1927	2	4
1927	Rabbit	Fire	Feb 2, 1927-Jan 22, 1928	1	5
1928	Dragon	Earth	Jan 23,1928- Feb 9, 1929	9	6
1929	Snake	Earth	Feb 10,1929 - Jan 29,1930	8	7
1930	Horse	Metal	Jan 30,1930- Feb 16 1931	7	8

KUA NUMBERS

YEAR OF BIRTH	ANIMAL SIGN	HEAVENLY STEM	BORN BETWEEN...	MEN	MEN
1931	Goat	Metal	Feb 17,1931 - Feb 5, 1932	6	9
1932	Monkey	Water	Feb 6, 1932-Jan 25,1933	5	1
1933	Rooster	Water	Jan 26, 1933-Feb 13, 1934	4	2
1934	Dog	Wood	Feb 14,1934- Feb 3,1935	3	3
1935	Pig	Wood	Feb 4, 1935-Jan 23, 1936	2	4
1936	Rat	Fire	Jan 24, 1936- Feb 10,1937	1	5
1937	Ox	Fire	Feb 11,1937-Jan 30,1938	9	6
1938	Tiger	Earth	Jan 31,1938-Feb 18, 1939	8	7
1939	Rabbit	Earth	Feb 19, 1939- Feb 7, 1940	7	8
1940	Dragon	Metal	Feb 8, 1940-Jan 26, 1941	6	9
1941	Snake	Metal	Jan 27, 1941 - Feb 14, 1942	5	1
1942	Horse	Water	Feb 15, 1942 - Feb 4,1943	4	2
1943	Goat	Water	Feb 5, 1943-Jan 24, 1944	3	3
1944	Monkey	Wood	Jan 25,1944-Feb 12,1945	2	4
1945	Rooster	Wood	Feb 13, 1945 - Feb 1, 1946	1	5
1946	Dog	Fire	Feb 2, 1946-Jan 21, 1947	9	6
1947	Pig	Fire	Jan 22, 1947-Feb 9, 1948	8	7
1948	Rat	Earth	Feb 10, 1948-Jan 28, 1949	7	8
1949	Ox	Earth	Jan 29, 1949-Feb 16, 1950	6	9
1950	Tiger	Metal	Feb 17, 1950- Feb 5,1951	5	1
1951	Rabbit	Metal	Feb 6, 1951 - Jan 26 1952	4	2
1952	Dragon	Water	Jan 27,1952 - Feb 13,1953	3	3
1953	Snake	Water	Feb 14, 1953- Feb 2, 1954	2	4
1954	Horse	Wood	Feb 3, 1954-Jan 23, 1955	1	5
1955	Goat	Wood	Jan 24, 1955-Feb 11, 1956	9	6
1956	Monkey	Fire	Feb 12,1956-Jan 30, 1957	8	7
1957	Rooster	Fire	Jan 31, 1957-Feb 17, 1958	7	8
1958	Dog	Earth	Feb 18, 1958-Feb 7 1959	6	9
1959	Pig	Earth	Feb 8, 1959-Jan 27, 1960	5	1
1960	Rat	Metal	Jan 28, 1960 - Feb 14, 1961	4	2
1961	Ox	Metal	Feb 15, 1961 - Feb 4, 1962	3	3

KUA NUMBERS

YEAR OF BIRTH	ANIMAL SIGN	HEAVENLY STEM	BORN BETWEEN...	MEN	MEN
1962	Tiger	Water	Feb 5, 1962 - Jan 24, 1963	2	4
1963	Rabbit	Water	Jan 25, 1963- Feb 12 1964	1	5
1964	Dragon	Wood	Feb 13, 1964-Feb 1,1965	9	6
1965	Snake	Wood	Feb 2, 1965-Jan 20, 1966	8	7
1966	Horse	Fire	Jan 21,1966-Feb 8,1967	7	8
1967	Goat	Fire	Feb 9,1967-Jan 29,1968	6	9
1968	Monkey	Earth	Jan 30, 1968-Feb 16, 1969	5	1
1969	Rooster	Earth	Feb 17, 1969-Feb 5, 1970	4	2
1970	Dog	Metal	Feb 6, 1970-Jan 26,1971	3	3
1971	Pig	Metal	Jan 27, 1971 - Feb 14, 1972	2	4
1972	Rat	Water	Feb 15, 1972-Feb 2, 1973	1	5
1973	Ox	Water	Feb 3, 1973-Jan 22, 1974	9	6
1974	Tiger	Wood	Jan 23, 1974-Feb 10, 1975	8	7
1975	Rabbit	Wood	Feb 11, 1975 - Jan 30, 1976	7	8
1976	Dragon	Fire	Jan 31, 1976-Feb 17 1977	6	9
1977	Snake	Fire	Feb 18,1977- Feb 6, 1978	5	1
1978	Horse	Earth	Feb 7, 1978 - Jan 27, 1979	4	2
1979	Goat	Earth	Jan 28, 1979 - Feb 15, 1980	3	3
1980	Monkey	Metal	Feb 16, 1980- Feb 4, 1981	2	4
1981	Rooster	Metal	Feb 5, 1981 - Jan 24, 1982	1	5
1982	Dog	Water	Jan 25, 1982-Feb12, 1983	9	6
1983	Pig	Water	Feb 13,1983- Feb 1,1984	8	7
1984	Rat	Wood	Feb 2,1984- Feb 19, 1985	7	8
1985	Ox	Wood	Feb 20, 1985-Feb 8, 1986	6	9
1986	Tiger	Fire	Feb 9, 1986-Jan 28, 1987	5	1
1987	Rabbit	Fire	Jan 29, 1987- Feb 16, 1988	4	2
1988	Dragon	Earth	Feb 17, 1988- Feb 5, 1989	3	3
1989	Snake	Earth	Feb 6, 1989-Jan 26, 1990	2	4
1990	Horse	Metal	Jan 27,1990 - Feb 14,1991	1	5
1991	Goat	Metal	Feb 15, 1991 - Feb 3, 1992	9	6
1992	Monkey	Water	Feb 4, 1992-Jan 22, 1993	8	7

KUA NUMBERS

YEAR OF BIRTH	ANIMAL SIGN	HEAVENLY STEM	BORN BETWEEN...	MEN	MEN
1993	Rooster	Water	Jan 23,1993 - Feb 9, 1994	7	8
1994	Dog	Wood	Feb 10, 1994-Jan 30, 1995	6	9
1995	Pig	Wood	Jan 31, 1995-Feb 18, 1996	5	1
1996	Rat	Fire	Feb 19, 1996 - Feb 6, 1997	4	2
1997	Ox	Fire	Feb 7, 1997 - Jan 27, 1998	3	3
1998	Tiger	Earth	Jan 28, 1998 - Feb 15,1999	2	4
1999	Rabbit	Earth	Feb 16, 1999-Feb 4, 2000	1	5
2000	Dragon	Metal	Feb 5, 2000 - Jan 23, 2001	9	6
2001	Snake	Metal	Jan 24, 2001 - Feb 11,2002	8	7
2002	Horse	Water	Feb 12, 2002-Jan 31,2003	7	8
2003	Goat	Water	Feb 1,2003 - Jan 21,2004	6	9
2004	Monkey	Wood	Jan 22, 2004 - Feb 8, 2005	5	1
2005	Rooster	Wood	Feb 9, 2005 - Jan 28, 2006	4	2
2006	Dog	Fire	Jan 29, 2006-Feb 17 2007	3	3
2007	Pig	Fire	Feb 18, 2007 - Feb 6, 2008	2	4
2008	Rat	Earth	Feb 7, 2008 - Jan 25, 2009	1	5
2009	Ox	Earth	Jan 26, 2009 - Feb 13, 2010	9	6
2010	Tiger	Metal	Feb 14, 2010-Feb 2, 2011	8	7
2011	Rabbit	Metal	Feb 3, 2011 - Jan 22, 2012	7	8
2012	Dragon	Water	Jan 23, 2012-Feb 9, 2013	6	9
2013	Snake	Water	Feb 10, 2013-Jan 30, 2014	5	1
2014	Horse	Wood	Jan 31,2014-Feb 18, 2015	4	2
2015	Goat	Wood	Feb 19, 2015-Feb 7, 2016	3	3
2016	Monkey	Fire	Feb 8, 2016-Jan 27,2017	2	4
2017	Rooster	Fire	Jan 28, 2017-Feb 15, 2018	1	5
2018	Dog	Earth	Feb 16, 2018-Feb 4, 2019	9	6
2019	Pig	Earth	Feb 5, 2019 - Jan 24, 2020	8	7
2020	Rat	Metal	Jan 25, 2020 - Feb 11,2021	7	8
2021	Ox	Metal	Feb 12, 2021 - Jan 31,2022	6	9
2022	Tiger	Water	Feb 1,2022-Jan 21,2023	5	1
2023	Rabbit	Water	Jan 22, 2023 - Feb 9, 2024	4	2

KUA NUMBERS

YEAR OF BIRTH	ANIMAL SIGN	HEAVENLY STEM	BORN BETWEEN...	MEN	MEN
2024	Dragon	Wood	Feb 10, 2024-Jan 28, 2025	3	3
2025	Snake	Wood	Jan 29, 2025-Feb 16, 2026	2	4
2026	Horse	Fire	Feb 17, 2026 - Feb 5, 2027	1	5
2027	Goat	Fire	Feb 6, 2027 - Jan 25, 2028	9	6
2028	Monkey	Earth	Jan 26, 2028 - Feb 12, 2029	8	7
2029	Rooster	Earth	Feb 13, 2029-Feb 2, 2030	7	8
2030	Dog	Metal	Feb 3, 2030 - Jan 22, 2031	6	9
2031	Pig	Metal	Jan 23, 2031 - Feb 10, 2032	5	1
2032	Rat	Water	Feb 11,2032-Jan 30, 2033	4	2
2033	Ox	Water	Jan 31,2033- Feb 18, 2034	3	3
2034	Tiger	Wood	Feb 19, 2034 - Feb 7 2035	2	4
2035	Rabbit	Wood	Feb 8, 2035 - Jan 27, 2036	1	5
2036	Dragon	Fire	Jan 28, 2036 - Feb 14, 2037	9	6
2037	Snake	Fire	Feb 15, 2037- Feb 3, 2038	8	7
2038	Horse	Earth	Feb 4, 2038 - Jan 23, 2039	7	8
2039	Goat	Earth	Jan 24, 2039 - Feb 11,2040	6	9
2040	Monkey	Metal	Feb 12, 2040-Jan 31,2041	5	1
2041	Rooster	Metal	Feb 1,2041 - Jan 21,2042	4	2
2042	Dog	Water	Jan 22, 2042 - Feb 9, 2043	3	3
2043	Pig	Water	Feb 10, 2043-Jan 29,2044	2	4
2044	Rat	Wood	Jan 30, 2044-Feb 16, 2045	1	5
2045	Ox	Wood	Feb 17, 2045 - Feb 5, 2046	9	6
2046	Tiger	Fire	Feb 6, 2046 - Jan 25, 2047	8	7
2047	Rabbit	Fire	Jan 26, 2047 - Feb 13, 2048	7	8
2048	Dragon	Earth	Feb 14, 2048 - Feb 1,2049	6	9
2049	Snake	Earth	Feb 2, 2049 - Jan 22, 2050	5	1
2050	Horse	Metal	Jan 23, 2050 - Feb 11,2051	4	2
2051	Goat	Metal	Feb 12, 2051 - Jan 31,2052	3	3
2052	Monkey	Water	Feb 1,2052-Feb 18, 2053	2	4
2053	Rooster	Water	Feb 19, 2053 - Feb 7, 2054	1	5
2054	Dog	Wood	Feb 8, 2054 - Jan 27, 2055	9	6

	AUSPICIOUS DIRECTIONS				INAUSPICIOUS DIRECTIONS			
	Sheng Chi **Direction: WEALTH**	Tien Yi **Direction: HEALTH**	Nien Yen **Direction: LOVE**	Fu Wei **Direction: PERSONAL GROWTH**	Ho Hai **Direction: BAD LUCK**	Wu Kwei **Direction: FIVE GHOSTS**	Lui Sha **Direction: SIX KILLINGS**	Chueh Ming **Direction: TOTAL LOSS**
Kua 1	Southeast	East	South	North	West	Northeast	Northwest	Southwest
Kua 2	Northeast	West	Northwest	Southwest	East	Southeast	South	North
Kua 3	South	North	Southeast	East	Southwest	Northwest	Northeast	West
Kua 4	North	South	East	Southeast	Northwest	Southwest	West	Northeast
Kua 4	For Kua 5 it becomes Kua 2 for males and Kua 8 for females							
Kua 6	West	Northeast	Southwest	Northwest	Southeast	East	North	South
Kua 7	Northwest	Southwest	Northeast	West	North	South	Southeast	East
Kua 8	Southwest	Northwest	West	Northeast	South	North	East	Southeast
Kua 9	East	Southeast	North	South	Northeast	West	Southwest	Northwest

Star Name		Characteristics
Sheng Chi	- Life Generating	Wealth, luck, political strength, authority, auspicious luck
Tien Yi	- Heavenly Doctor	Good health, noble people luck
Nien Yen	- Longevity	Good relationships, smooth sailing, good networking
Fu Wei	- Stability	Calmness, steadiness, soothing
Ho Hai	- Mishaps	Obstacles, hindrance, negative setbacks
Wu Kwei	- 5 Ghosts	Gossip, backstabbing, sabotage, ill health
Lui Sha	- 6 Killings	Betrayal, accidents, lawsuits
Chueh Ming	-Total Loss	Catastrophe, major problems, life threatening issues

YOUR PERSONAL KUA DIRECTIONS

Name...
Date of Birth...
Kua Number..
Kua Element..

Best Direction	1	2	3	4
	Life	Health	Longevity	Stability
	Wealth	Noble people	Study	Abundance
	Success		Relationships	Wellbeing
Unlucky Directions	5	6	7	8
	Mishaps	Obstacles	Difficulty	Loss
	Misfortune	Ill Heath	betrayal	Total loss
	Accidents	Burglary	Legal dealings	Bad health

Chinese Astrology Sign..Element..

BEST DIRECTION

Wealth and Success...

Health...

Desk – Business - Study..

Sleep and Relationships..

DIRECTION TO AVOID

Bed head & Front door...

THE FOUR CELESTIAL GUARDIANS

Dressing tables should not face the bed directly. The mirror will cause bad luck and friction in relationships.

Traditional blues and greys bring a very calm coastal feel to a home's energy... be mindful when decorating in this style that the space does not become and feel too cold or emotions will be strong... strengthen and balance with plants and pop of fire by implimenting candles and bright lights...

Display Goldfish for luck. An excellent way to activated energy inside the home is with 9 goldfish in an aquarium or art system.

Warm up the bedroom, add a splash of blush, pink, purple, maroon, plum or red... the bedroom needs to be inviting and represents what you want out of your relationship... red adds passion...

The most auspicious location for your home is determined by the position of the four celestial guardians, which form an armchair configeration.

The Black Turtle is represented by mountains or hills behind the home.

These hills should be higher to act as support and protection for the residents.

The Green Dragon is represented by rolling hills to the left of the home. These hills should be higher than hills to the right of the home.

The White Tiger is represented by hills to the right of the home. Hills to the right should be lower than the left.

The Crimson Phoenix should be a hillock and found in fron of the home. This represents a footstool.

If the configeration of your land is not ideal, you can improve your feng shui by placing images of the four celestial guardians to symbolise their presence in the home.

SPECIAL ANIMAL PAIRINGS

Different to your secret friend and your allies, there are other animal's pairings which are formed based on the order of appearance of the animals on the compass. These pairings bring diverse types of energy when they come together.

Rat and Ox: The Rat is Yang and the Ox is Yin. The Rat initiates, the Ox completes. Together they create inspiration and ingenuity.

Tigger and Rabbit: The Tiger is Yang and the Rabbit is Yin. The Tiger employs force, the Rabbit uses diplomacy. Together they create growth and development.

Dragon and Snake: The Dragon is Yang and the Snake is Yin. The Dragon creates magic, the Snake creates mystery. Together they create magic and spirituality.

Horse and Goat: The Horse is Yang and the Goat is Yin. The Horse embodies male energy, the Goat embodies female energy. Together they create passion and sexuality.

Monkey and Rooster: The Monkey is Yang and the Rooster is Yin. The Monkey creates strategy and the Rooster gets things moving. Together they create career and commerce.

Dog and Pig: The Dog is Yang and the Pig is Yin. The Dog works to provide, the Pig enjoys what is created. Together they create domesticity.

01 | 2022 January

THE WATER TIGER YEAR

3 monday

Animal: **fire dragon**
Flying Star: **2**
Good day: **rat, monkey**
Bad day: **dog**

4 tuesday

Animal: **fire snake**
Flying Star: **3**
Good day: **ox, rooster**
Bad day: **pig**

5 wednesday

Animal: **earth horse**
Flying Star: **4**
Good day: **tiger, dog**
Bad day: **rat**

6 thursday

Animal: **earth goat**
Flying Star: **5**
Good day: **rabbit, pig**
Bad day: **ox**

7 friday

Animal: **metal monkey**
Flying Star: **6**
Good day: **rat, dragon**
Bad day: **tiger**

8 saturday

Animal: **metal rooster**
Flying Star: **7**
Good day: **ox, snake**
Bad day: **rabbit**

9 sunday

Animal: **water dog**
Flying Star: **8**
Good day: **tiger, horse**
Bad day: **dragon**

JANUARY 2022

OX

(1925, 1937, 1949, 1961, 1973, 1985, 1997, 2009, 2021)

The hardest worker of all the animals; they are persistent, will take the pressure off others, have a high stamina, and will carry heavy burdens. But ... they can be stubborn, reveal very little, including their health and will seldom complain. They also tend to stay put for extended periods of time.

Favourable monthly animal - rat, snake, rooster

Unfavourable monthly animal - goat

01 2022 January

THE WATER TIGER YEAR

10 monday
Animal: **water pig**
Flying Star: **9**
Good day: **rabbit, goat**
Bad day: **snake**

11 tuesday
Animal: **wood rat**
Flying Star: **1**
Good day: **dragon, monkey**
Bad day: **horse**

12 wednesday
Animal: **wood ox**
Flying Star: **2**
Good day: **snake, rooster**
Bad day: **goat**

13 thursday
Animal: **fire tiger**
Flying Star: **3**
Good day: **rhorse, dog**
Bad day: **monkey**

14 friday
Animal: **fire rabbit**
Flying Star: **4**
Good day: **goat, pig**
Bad day: **rooster**

15 saturday
Animal: **earth dragon**
Flying Star: **5**
Good day: **rat, monkey**
Bad day: **dog**

16 sunday
Animal: **earth snake**
Flying Star: **6**
Good day: **ox, rooster**
Bad day: **pig**

For January, the monthly visiting **Flying Star 3** brings **gossip, arguments, legal trouble, conflict, and disputes**.

It is a hostile Star, known for bringing about violence, anger, misunderstandings, constant disagreements, heated arguments, litigation, trouble with authorities and in extreme cases, legal complications between family members, friends and or colleagues.

Health issues related to the liver, gall bladder, feet and arms may arise. As the yearly flying star sits in the Southwest and the Southwest belongs to the earth element. Wood controls the earth so there will also be earth related issues such as digestive problems. Productivity will drop. Relationships between spouses will be affected with high tense energies. Harmony of families and stability of marriages will also be affected. Watch out for trouble with the authorities or you may be hit with litigation. The matriarch, older women, Monkey and Goat born people are the most likely to be affected this month.

Cures to be placed for January include a red piece of paper which is the traditional Chinese cure, or other red and purple décor objects. This includes candles, or bright lights. A magic flaming wheel can be used, or an image of a red phoenix or an eagle. If your front door is in the Southwest sector, you would benefit greatly by placing temple lions there for extra protection along with an evil eye symbol.

Pertaining to the Luo Shu or Bagua school of Feng Shui, the annual flying star 3 sits in the Southwest sector for 2022 this sector is representative of relationship luck, love, romance, and marriage.

The Southwest belongs to the element of earth, to enhance the Southwest of your home for positive relationship luck. Use earth and fire energy for support; amethyst, rose quartz crystal, or purple, pink, red peonies. Also, the double happiness symbol, a pair of Mandarin Ducks is symbolism of couples. Additional bright lights are recommended in this sector.

01 | 2022 January

THE WATER TIGER YEAR

17 monday

Animal: **metal horse**
Flying Star: **7**
Good day: **tiger, dog**
Bad day: **rat**

18 tuesday

Animal: **metal goat**
Flying Star: **8**
Good day: **rabbit, pig**
Bad day: **ox**

19 wednesday

Animal: **water monkey**
Flying Star: **9**
Good day: **rat, dragon**
Bad day: **tiger**

20 thursday

Animal: **water rooster**
Flying Star: **1**
Good day: **ox, snake**
Bad day: **rabbit**

21 friday

Animal: **wood dog**
Flying Star: **2**
Good day: **tiger, horse**
Bad day: **dragon**

22 saturday

Animal: **wood pig**
Flying Star: **3**
Good day: **rabbit, goat**
Bad day: **snake**

23 sunday

Animal: **fire rat**
Flying Star: **4**
Good day: **dragon, monkey**
Bad day: **horse**

Happy Family Luck. Place family portraits in the Southwest or West. Or facing South, Southwest or Northwest.

01 | 2022 January

THE WATER TIGER YEAR

24 monday

Animal: **Fire ox**
Flying Star: **5**
Good day: **snake, rooster**
Bad day: **goat**

25 tuesday

Animal: **earth tiger**
Flying Star: **6**
Good day: **horse, dog**
Bad day: **monkey**

26 wednesday

Animal: **earth rabbit**
Flying Star: **7**
Good day: **goat, pig**
Bad day: **rooster**

27 thursday

Animal: **metal dragon**
Flying Star: **8**
Good day: **rat, monkey**
Bad day: **dog**

28 friday

Animal: **metal snake**
Flying Star: **9**
Good day: **ox, rooster**
Bad day: **pig**

29 saturday

Animal: **water horse**
Flying Star: **1**
Good day: **tiger, dog**
Bad day: **rat**

30 sunday

Animal: **water goat**
Flying Star: **2**
Good day: **rabbit, pig**
Bad day: **ox**

02 | 2022 February

THE WATER TIGER YEAR

31 monday

Animal: **wood monkey**
Flying Star: **3**
Good day: **rat, dragon**
Bad day: **tiger**

1 tuesday

Chinese new year

Animal: **wood rooster**
Flying Star: **4**
Good day: **ox, snake**
Bad day: **rabbit**

2 wednesday

Animal: **fire dog**
Flying Star: **5**
Good day: **tiger, horse**
Bad day: **dragon**

3 thursday

Animal: **fire pig**
Flying Star: **6**
Good day: **rabbit, goat**
Bad day: **snake**

4 friday

Animal: **earth rat**
Flying Star: **7**
Good day: **dragon, monkey**
Bad day: **horse**

5 saturday

Animal: **earth ox**
Flying Star: **8**
Good day: **snake, rooster**
Bad day: **goat**

6 sunday

Animal: **metal tiger**
Flying Star: **9**
Good day: **horse, dog**
Bad day: **monkey**

FEBRUARY 2022

TIGER

(1926, 1938, 1950, 1962, 1974, 1986, 1998, 2010, 2022)

Sensitive, alert, has a lot of energy, influential and can be bad tempered. They are usually leaders, take chances and lead fortunate lives. They are also independent and fiercely protective of their family.

Favourable monthly animal - Pig, Horse, Dog

Unfavourable monthly animal - Monkey

02 | 2022 February

THE WATER TIGER YEAR

7 monday
Animal: **metal rabbit**
Flying Star: **1**
Good day: **goat, pig**
Bad day: **rooster**

8 tuesday
Animal: **water dragon**
Flying Star: **2**
Good day: **rat, monkey**
Bad day: **dog**

9 wednesday
Animal: **water snake**
Flying Star: **3**
Good day: **ox, rooster**
Bad day: **pig**

10 thursday
Animal: **wood horse**
Flying Star: **4**
Good day: **tiger, dog**
Bad day: **rat**

11 friday
Animal: **wood goat**
Flying Star: **5**
Good day: **rabbit, pig**
Bad day: **ox**

12 saturday
Animal: **fire monkey**
Flying Star: **6**
Good day: **rat, dragon**
Bad day: **tiger**

13 sunday
Animal: **fire rooster**
Flying Star: **7**
Good day: **ox, snake**
Bad day: **rabbit**

For February, the monthly visiting **Flying Star 2** brings **turbulent energies, negative people, illness, sickness, disease and stress** to all homes and businesses.

It is an Earth element Star that threatens to bring turbulent energies wreaking havoc on health, illness, disease, and those with existing or persistent health problems. It is believed to worsen an existing illness. In 2022, women, elderly women and pregnant women will be affected by this negative Star the most. In 2022, it will affect you if your front door, main bedroom or living area is in the Southwest; or the Monkey and Goat born person, will experience feeling physically and mentally weak. The flying star 2 has the potential to bring positive property related or real estate investments but it will come at the cost of health.

It is strongly advised to help cure the Southwest of your home and business with a **health gourd**, (also known as a wu lou), six gold coins on red tassel, a saltwater cure, and a Quan yin. If possible, wear a wu lou pendant or carry a wu lou amulet if you are a Monkey or Goat. A metal bell or windchime, can be used but the metal energy is to be reasonably still and heavy, so metal wall sculptures work better.

To counter the effects of this negative star, place heavy metal objects made of brass, cooper, bronze, or pewter in this sector. Metallic artwork, colours, white, silver, gold, and home décor items. Reduce and remove Fire and earth energy.

Pertaining to the Luo Shu or Bagua school of Feng Shui, the annual flying star 2 sits in the Southwest sector for 2022 this sector is representative of relationship luck, love, romance, and marriage.

The Southwest belongs to the element of earth, to support aspects of the Southwest of your home for positive relationship luck. Use pink and red peonies, a double happiness symbol, a pair of Mandarin Ducks, and or symbolism of couples in this sector.

02 | 2022 February

THE WATER TIGER YEAR

14 monday
Animal: **earth dog**
Flying Star: **8**
Good day: **tiger, horse**
Bad day: **dragon**

15 tuesday
Animal: **earth pig**
Flying Star: **9**
Good day: **rabbit, goat**
Bad day: **snake**

16 wednesday
Animal: **metal rat**
Flying Star: **1**
Good day: **dragon, monkey**
Bad day: **horse**

17 thursday
Animal: **metal ox**
Flying Star: **2**
Good day: **snake, rooster**
Bad day: **goat**

18 friday
Animal: **water tiger**
Flying Star: **3**
Good day: **horse, dog**
Bad day: **monkey**

19 saturday
Animal: **water rabbit**
Flying Star: **4**
Good day: **goat, pig**
Bad day: **rooster**

20 sunday
Animal: **wood dragon**
Flying Star: **5**
Good day: **rat, monkey**
Bad day: **dog**

Display Peonies for Love. It is believed the peony keeps romance and love alive.

02 | 2022 February

THE WATER TIGER YEAR

21 monday
Animal: **wood snake**
Flying Star: **6**
Good day: **ox, rooster**
Bad day: **pig**

22 tuesday
Animal: **fire horse**
Flying Star: **7**
Good day: **tiger, dog**
Bad day: **rat**

23 wednesday
Animal: **fire goat**
Flying Star: **8**
Good day: **rabbit, pig**
Bad day: **ox**

24 thursday
Animal: **earth monkey**
Flying Star: **9**
Good day: **rat, dragon**
Bad day: **tiger**

25 friday
Animal: **earth rooster**
Flying Star: **1**
Good day: **ox, snake**
Bad day: **rabbit**

26 saturday
Animal: **metal dog**
Flying Star: **2**
Good day: **tiger, horse**
Bad day: **dragon**

27 sunday
Animal: **metal pig**
Flying Star: **3**
Good day: **rabbit, goat**
Bad day: **snake**

03 | 2022 March

THE WATER TIGER YEAR

28 monday
Animal: **water rat**
Flying Star: **4**
Good day: **dragon, monkey**
Bad day: **horse**

1 tuesday
Animal: **water ox**
Flying Star: **5**
Good day: **snake, rooster**
Bad day: **goat**

2 wednesday
Animal: **wood tiger**
Flying Star: **6**
Good day: **horse, dog**
Bad day: **monkey**

3 thursday
Animal: **wood rabbit**
Flying Star: **7**
Good day: **goat, pig**
Bad day: **rooster**
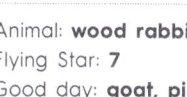

4 friday
Animal: **fire dragon**
Flying Star: **8**
Good day: **rat, monkey**
Bad day: **dog**

5 saturday
Animal: **fire snake**
Flying Star: **9**
Good day: **ox, rooster**
Bad day: **pig**

6 sunday
Animal: **earth horse**
Flying Star: **1**
Good day: **tiger, dog**
Bad day: **rat**

MARCH 2022

RABBIT

(1915, 1927, 1939, 1951, 1963, 1975, 1987, 1999, 2011, 2023)

Exceptionally sensitive, alert, intelligent and honest. Their minds move at great speeds, they are clever, analytical and will always have back up plans. They are soft, emotional, sensitive and quick tempered, but very rarely express it. They can be impatient, vulnerable and believe it or not, they are a great asset to have.

Favourable monthly animal = Dog, Goat and Pig

Unfavourable monthly animal = Rooster

03 | 2022 March

THE WATER TIGER YEAR

7 monday
Animal: **earth goat**
Flying Star: **2**
Good day: **rabbit, pig**
Bad day: **ox**

8 tuesday
Animal: **metal monkey**
Flying Star: **3**
Good day: **rat, dragon**
Bad day: **tiger**

9 wednesday
Animal: **metal rooster**
Flying Star: **4**
Good day: **ox, snake**
Bad day: **rabbit**

10 thursday
Animal: **water dog**
Flying Star: **5**
Good day: **tiger, horse**
Bad day: **dragon**

11 friday
Animal: **water pig**
Flying Star: **6**
Good day: **rabbit, goat**
Bad day: **snake**

12 saturday
Animal: **wood rat**
Flying Star: **7**
Good day: **dragon, monkey**
Bad day: **horse**

13 sunday
Animal: **wood ox**
Flying Star: **8**
Good day: **snake, rooster**
Bad day: **goat**

For March, the monthly visiting **Flying Star 1**, known as the **Star of Triumph, fame, wealth, intelligence, and Success**, brings positive energies. This lucky Star is associated with winning attaining success, reputation, good name, status, and fame. It brings excellent triumphant victory over competition, career, and academic pursuits such as writing / research and scholastic success. This lucky star derives remarkable success for wealth opportunities, networking and social circles promoting reputation with influence and victory. This month will effectively enhance noble pursuits, as well as wealth or career related pursuits especially if you are a teen boy Rat born person. Those who enjoy these good influences will be inclined to experience competitive activities.

The Flying Star 1 has a positive influence in attracting victory over past malaise and niggling health concerns. But it is wise to watch out for emotional turbulences such as emotional instability and depression can occur. The Water element brings triumph via Yang energy to this auspicious Star, which you can activate by placing metal objects, like a windchime, or your collection of trophies and medals. A water feature or a Victory Horse figurine and a Ruyi in this sector is also suggested.

Pertaining to the Luo Shu or Bagua school of Feng Shui, the annual flying star 1 sits in the North sector for 2022 this sector is representative of career and business luck.

The North belongs to the element of Water. To enhance the North of your home for career and business support and luck, place metal colours like white, silver, gold, pewter, bronze and black to support the water energy, or metal decor objects, with blue black tones or water pictures and décor items. A Black Tortoise or Dragon Tortoise piece can also be used.

03 | 2022 March

THE WATER TIGER YEAR

14 monday

Animal: **fire tiger**
Flying Star: **9**
Good day: **horse, dog**
Bad day: **monkey**

15 tuesday

Animal: **fire rabbit**
Flying Star: **1**
Good day: **goat, pig**
Bad day: **rooster**

16 wednesday

Animal: **earth dragon**
Flying Star: **2**
Good day: **rat, monkey**
Bad day: **dog**

17 thursday

Animal: **earth snake**
Flying Star: **3**
Good day: **ox, rooster**
Bad day: **pig**

18 friday

Animal: **metal horse**
Flying Star: **4**
Good day: **tiger, dog**
Bad day: **rat**

19 saturday

Animal: **metal goat**
Flying Star: **5**
Good day: **rabbit, pig**
Bad day: **ox**

20 sunday

Animal: **water monkey**
Flying Star: **6**
Good day: **rat, dragon**
Bad day: **tiger**

Water in the North of your home is supportive for career and business luck. Water flow should always flow towards the home and not away, water should be clean clear but not stagnant. Fish are great for keeping the water moving and clean. The number of fish and kind is not as important as clean flowing water... Koi are a popular Chinese fish choice...

03 | 2022 March

THE WATER TIGER YEAR

21 monday
Animal: **water rooster**
Flying Star: **7**
Good day: **ox, snake**
Bad day: **rabbit**

22 tuesday
Animal: **wood dog**
Flying Star: **8**
Good day: **tiger, horse**
Bad day: **dragon**

23 wednesday
Animal: **wood pig**
Flying Star: **9**
Good day: **rabbit, goat**
Bad day: **snake**

24 thursday
Animal: **fire rat**
Flying Star: **1**
Good day: **dragon, monkey**
Bad day: **horse**

25 friday
Animal: **fire ox**
Flying Star: **2**
Good day: **snake, rooster**
Bad day: **goat**

26 saturday
Animal: **earth tiger**
Flying Star: **3**
Good day: **horse, dog**
Bad day: **monkey**

27 sunday
Animal: **earth rabbit**
Flying Star: **4**
Good day: **goat, pig**
Bad day: **rooster**

ACTIVATING FENG SHUI IN THE GARDEN

Each sector of the Ba Gua has an element. You can use the productive cycle to enhance the element that represents that sector of the garden. Use the colour of the flowers to symbolically create the presence of these elements.

SOUTHEAST

The element of SMALL WOOD is associated with the colour light GREEN, young growing plants, anything rectangular, the season of Spring Sc expanding energy.

SOUTH

The element of FIRE is associated with the colour RED, bright sunlight, the glow of lamps, anything sharp or pointed, the season of Summer and upwards rising energy.

SOUTHWEST

The element of BIG EARTH is associated with the colour of OCHRE, stones and pebbles, boulders and crystals, in between seasons 8c sideways moving energy.

EAST

The element of BIG WOOD is associated with the colour dark green, full grown plants, flowers and seeds, the season of Spring 8c outwards flowing energy.

THE CENTER IS OF THE EARTH ELEMENT

WEST

The element of SMALL METAL is associated with white, gold and silver, the season of Autumn, 8c inward flowing energy.

NORTHEAST

The element of SMALL EARTH is associated with the colour beige, the soil, the earth, anything square, in between seasons 8c horizontal moving energy.

NORTH

The element of WATER is associated with the colours black/blue, the season of Winter, anything wavy in shape 8c meandering energy.

NORTHWEST

The element of BIG METAL is associated with all metallic colours, gold and silver, the season of Autumn 8c inward flowing energy.

03 | 2022 March

THE WATER TIGER YEAR

28 monday

Animal: **metal dragon**
Flying Star: **5**
Good day: **rat, monkey**
Bad day: **dog**

29 tuesday

Animal: **metal snake**
Flying Star: **6**
Good day: **ox, rooster**
Bad day: **pig**

30 wednesday

Animal: **water horse**
Flying Star: **7**
Good day: **tiger, dog**
Bad day: **rat**

31 thursday

Animal: **water goat**
Flying Star: **8**
Good day: **rabbit, pig**
Bad day: **ox**

1 friday

Animal: **wood monkey**
Flying Star: **9**
Good day: **rat, dragon**
Bad day: **tiger**

2 saturday

Animal: **wood rooster**
Flying Star: **1**
Good day: **ox, snake**
Bad day: **rabbit**

3 sunday

Animal: **fire dog**
Flying Star: **2**
Good day: **tiger, horse**
Bad day: **dragon**

04 | 2022 April

THE WATER TIGER YEAR

4 monday

Animal: **fire pig**
Flying Star: **3**
Good day: **rabbit, sheep**
Bad day: **snake**

5 tuesday

Animal: **earth rat**
Flying Star: **4**
Good day: **dragon, monkey**
Bad day: **horse**

6 wednesday

Animal: **earth ox**
Flying Star: **5**
Good day: **snake, rooster**
Bad day: **goat**

7 thursday

Animal: **metal tiger**
Flying Star: **6**
Good day: **horse, dog**
Bad day: **monkey**

8 friday

Animal: **metal rabbit**
Flying Star: **7**
Good day: **goat, pig**
Bad day: **rooster**

9 saturday

Animal: **water dragon**
Flying Star: **8**
Good day: **rat, monkey**
Bad day: **dog**

10 sunday

Animal: **water snake**
Flying Star: **9**
Good day: **ox, rooster**
Bad day: **pig**

APRIL 2022

DRAGON

(1916, 1928, 1940, 1952, 1964, 1976, 1988, 2000, 2012, 2024)

Spirit of great power, wisdom, strength and energy. They can look down on people, but they work and accomplish on grand scale. A love for challenges, in order to gain respect and support of others. They are dreamers, creative, optimistic, steady and firm. Dragons are generally very good in business.

Favourable monthly animal = Rooster, Rat, Monkey

Unfavourable monthly animal = Dog

04 | 2022 April

THE WATER TIGER YEAR

11 monday
Animal: **wood horse**
Flying Star: **1**
Good day: **tiger, dog**
Bad day: **rat**

12 tuesday
Animal: **wood goat**
Flying Star: **2**
Good day: **rabbit, horse**
Bad day: **ox**

13 wednesday
Animal: **fire monkey**
Flying Star: **3**
Good day: **rat, dragon**
Bad day: **tiger**

14 thursday
Animal: **fire rooster**
Flying Star: **4**
Good day: **ox, snake**
Bad day: **rabbit**

15 friday
Animal: **earth dog**
Flying Star: **5**
Good day: **tiger, horse**
Bad day: **dragon**

16 saturday
Animal: **earth pig**
Flying Star: **6**
Good day: **rabbit, goat**
Bad day: **snake**

17 sunday
Animal: **metal rat**
Flying Star: **7**
Good day: **dragon, monkey**
Bad day: **horse**

For April, the monthly visiting **Flying Star 9** shines brightly. It is the **Star of Future Prosperity, Completion, fame, celebration, wealth intelligence and popularity**, happiness, and recognition. This dynamic and entertaining Fire Star spurs celebrations, festivities, gatherings, and excellent good luck. It is also referred to as the Star of completion because it shows the ability to bring successful fruition to projects started previously. There is notable success in finance and an abundance of luck. It enhances the luck to positive outcomes in the future for the seeds you have previously sown and encourages any endeavour towards boosting your income; especially if you are a teen girl, or Horse born person.

This is also a secondary Star that brings wealth, with boosts to business profits and investments. A raise of fame and recognition. Some believe the Flying Star 9 is more powerful and potent than the Flying Star 8. You are advised to use this space frequently if you wish to start a new business, plan to marry or start a family. Enhance with any wealth symbolism such as a wealth jar, Buddha, trinity of horses, 9 Gold Coins on tassel, a Wealth God or Gold Ingots, objects in multiples of nine and keep this part of the home or office brightly lit. Red phoenix, lots of red upholstery and decor here. Nine fish in water an excellent energy enhancer.

Pertaining to the Luo Shu or Bagua school of Feng Shui, the annual flying star 9 sits in the South sector for 2022, this sector is representative of fame, recognition, and reputation.

The South belongs to the element of Fire, to enhance the South of your home for recognition. The South sector is the home of the celestial red phoenix, to triumph over competition with opportunities use the statue of Phoenix or a horse picture or statue to bring speed and endurance in your endeavours. Generally bright lights and objects of red (fire) colours are the most auspicious in the South. Add more wood element such as plants to balance water and fire energy. Galloping Horses or Horse symbolism are the best enhancement.

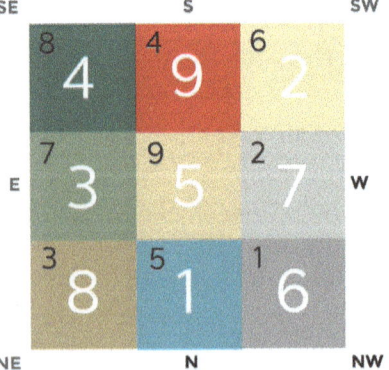

04 | 2022 April

THE WATER TIGER YEAR

18 monday
Animal: **metal ox**
Flying Star: **8**
Good day: **snake, rabbit**
Bad day: **goat**

19 tuesday
Animal: **water tiger**
Flying Star: **9**
Good day: **horse, dog**
Bad day: **monkey**

20 wednesday
Animal: **water rabbit**
Flying Star: **1**
Good day: **tiger, horse**
Bad day: **rooster**

21 thursday
Animal: **wood dragon**
Flying Star: **2**
Good day: **rat, monkey**
Bad day: **dog**

22 friday
Animal: **wood snake**
Flying Star: **3**
Good day: **ox, rabbit**
Bad day: **pig**

23 saturday
Animal: **fire horse**
Flying Star: **4**
Good day: **tiger, dog**
Bad day: **rat**

24 sunday
Animal: **fire goat**
Flying Star: **5**
Good day: **rabbit, pig**
Bad day: **ox**

Play loud music once a week. To clear old energies and welcome in new...

04 | 2022 April

THE WATER TIGER YEAR

25 monday
Animal: **earth monkey**
Flying Star: **6**
Good day: **ox, rooster**
Bad day: **tiger**

26 tuesday
Animal: **earth rooster**
Flying Star: **7**
Good day: **ox, snake**
Bad day: **dog**

27 wednesday
Animal: **metal dog**
Flying Star: **8**
Good day: **tiger, horse**
Bad day: **dragon**

28 thursday
Animal: **metal pig**
Flying Star: **9**
Good day: **rabbit, goat**
Bad day: **snake**

29 friday
Animal: **water rat**
Flying Star: **1**
Good day: **dragon, monkey**
Bad day: **horse**

30 saturday
Animal: **water ox**
Flying Star: **2**
Good day: **snake, rooster**
Bad day: **goat**

1 sunday
Animal: **wood tiger**
Flying Star: **3**
Good day: **horse, dog**
Bad day: **monkey**

05 | 2022 May

THE WATER TIGER YEAR

2 monday
Animal: **wood rabbit**
Flying Star: **4**
Good day: **goat, pig**
Bad day: **rooster**

3 tuesday
Animal: **fire dragon**
Flying Star: **5**
Good day: **rat, monkey**
Bad day: **dog**

4 wednesday
Animal: **fire snake**
Flying Star: **6**
Good day: **ox, rooster**
Bad day: **pig**

5 thursday
Animal: **earth horse**
Flying Star: **7**
Good day: **tiger, dog**
Bad day: **rat**

6 friday
Animal: **earth goat**
Flying Star: **8**
Good day: **rabbit, pig**
Bad day: **ox**

7 saturday
Animal: **metal monkey**
Flying Star: **9**
Good day: **rat, dragon**
Bad day: **tiger**

8 sunday
Animal: **metal rooster**
Flying Star: **1**
Good day: **ox, snake**
Bad day: **rabbit**

MAY 2022

SNAKE

(1917, 1929, 1941, 1953, 1965, 1977, 1989, 2001, 2013)

Has sensitivity, very perceptive, alert and enjoys life to the full. Goal orientated, persistent, alert, loyal, patient, but unforgiving; do not make them your enemy, but they make great friends. Snakes tend to acquire knowledge and then move on. They are determined and can be wise.

Favourable monthly animal -Monkey, Ox, Rooster

Unfavourable monthly animal - Pig

05 | 2022 May

THE WATER TIGER YEAR

9 monday

Animal: **water dog**
Flying Star: **2**
Good day: **tiger, horse**
Bad day: **dragon**

10 tuesday

Animal: **water pig**
Flying Star: **3**
Good day: **rabbit, goat**
Bad day: **snake**

11 wednesday

Animal: **wood rat**
Flying Star: **4**
Good day: **dragon, monkey**
Bad day: **horse**

12 thursday

Animal: **wood ox**
Flying Star: **5**
Good day: **snake, rooster**
Bad day: **goat**

13 friday

Animal: **fire tiger**
Flying Star: **6**
Good day: **horse, dog**
Bad day: **monkey**

14 saturday

Animal: **fire rabbit**
Flying Star: **7**
Good day: **goat, pig**
Bad day: **rooster**

15 sunday

Animal: **earth dragon**
Flying Star: **8**
Good day: **rat, monkey**
Bad day: **dog**

For May, the monthly visiting **Flying Star 8** shines bright. It is the **Star of wealth, health, prosperity, fame, finance, and current prosperity** bringing abundant wealth, money, fortune and good luck of wealth, nobility, and steadfastness. You can expect improved income, wealth success and power luck. Professional pursuits, good reputation and efforts acknowledged will flourish if you can tap into this positive month.

If your home has a Northeast main door, living or family area in this sector, everyone in your home will be able to gain from this Star throughout May. Especially if you are a young boy, Ox or Tiger born person.

To allow energy to flow, this area should be kept clutter-free. To activate its luck, any form of wealth symbolism can be placed in this area such as a Buddha, 6 Gold Coins on tassel, a Wealth God or Gold Ingots, as well as bright lights clocks, TV and lots of activity. Remember movement or your footsteps are the most powerful mover of energy.

Pertaining to the Luo Shu or Bagua School of Feng Shui, the annual flying star 8 sits in the North-East sector for 2022, this sector is representative of knowledge, scholarly, learning and education.

The Northeast belongs to the element of Earth, so this is an auspicious location. To support and enhance use a picture of Mountains, a Crystal Globe, world map, Chinese saint Luohan or Dragon Carp. Take note if the North-East sector is blocked by a large tree or missing space, you will have trouble tapping into learning and knowledge.

05 | 2022 May

THE WATER TIGER YEAR

16 monday
Animal: **earth snake**
Flying Star: **9**
Good day: **ox, rooster**
Bad day: **pig**

17 tuesday
Animal: **metal horse**
Flying Star: **1**
Good day: **tiger dog**
Bad day: **rat**

18 wednesday
Animal: **metal goat**
Flying Star: **2**
Good day: **rabbit, pig**
Bad day: **ox**

19 thursday
Animal: **water monkey**
Flying Star: **3**
Good day: **rat, dragon**
Bad day: **tiger**

20 friday
Animal: **water rooster**
Flying Star: **4**
Good day: **ox, snake**
Bad day: **rabbit**

21 saturday
Animal: **wood dog**
Flying Star: **5**
Good day: **tiger, horse**
Bad day: **dragon**

22 sunday
Animal: **wood pig**
Flying Star: **6**
Good day: **rabbit, goat**
Bad day: **snake**

Fire and Water should not clash in a kitchen. Sink and Stove should not be next to each other or opposite.

05 | 2022 May

THE WATER TIGER YEAR

23 monday

Animal: **fire rat**
Flying Star: **7**
Good day: **dragon, monkey**
Bad day: **horse**

24 tuesday

Animal: **fire ox**
Flying Star: **8**
Good day: **snake, rooster**
Bad day: **goat**

25 wednesday

Animal: **earth tiger**
Flying Star: **9**
Good day: **horse, dog**
Bad day: **monkey**

26 thursday

Animal: **earth rabbit**
Flying Star: **1**
Good day: **goat, pig**
Bad day: **rooster**

27 friday

Animal: **metal dragon**
Flying Star: **2**
Good day: **rat, monkey**
Bad day: **dog**

28 saturday

Animal: **metal snake**
Flying Star: **3**
Good day: **ox, rooster**
Bad day: **pig**

29 sunday

Animal: **water horse**
Flying Star: **4**
Good day: **tiger, dog**
Bad day: **rat**

06 | 2022 June

THE WATER TIGER YEAR

30 monday
Animal: **water goat**
Flying Star: **5**
Good day: **rabbit, pig**
Bad day: **ox**

31 tuesday
Animal: **wood monkey**
Flying Star: **6**
Good day: **rat, dragon**
Bad day: **tiger**

1 wednesday
Animal: **wood rooster**
Flying Star: **7**
Good day: **ox, snake**
Bad day: **rabbit**

2 thursday
Animal: **fire dog**
Flying Star: **8**
Good day: **tiger, horse**
Bad day: **dragon**

3 friday
Animal: **fire pig**
Flying Star: **9**
Good day: **rabbit, goat**
Bad day: **snake**

4 saturday
Animal: **earth rat**
Flying Star: **1**
Good day: **dragon, monkey**
Bad day: **horse**

5 sunday
Animal: **earth ox**
Flying Star: **2**
Good day: **snake, rooster**
Bad day: **goat**

JUNE 2022

HORSE

(1918, 1930, 1942, 1954, 1966, 1978, 1990, 2002. 2014)

Devoted, have inner-strength, persistent, hard workers and determined. They are dependable, honest, and loyal and love challenges. They are proud, independent, but they need companions. Horse's also likes the comforts can be frivolous and love to gossip.

Favourable monthly animal - Goat, Tiger, Pig

Unfavourable monthly animal - Rat

06 | 2022 June

THE WATER TIGER YEAR

6 monday
Animal: **metal tiger**
Flying Star: **3**
Good day: **horse, dog**
Bad day: **monkey**

7 tuesday
Animal: **metal rabbit**
Flying Star: **4**
Good day: **goat, pig**
Bad day: **rooster**

8 wednesday
Animal: **water dragon**
Flying Star: **5**
Good day: **rat, monkey**
Bad day: **dog**

9 thursday
Animal: **water snake**
Flying Star: **6**
Good day: **ox, rooster**
Bad day: **pig**

10 friday
Animal: **wood horse**
Flying Star: **7**
Good day: **tiger, dog**
Bad day: **rat**

11 saturday
Animal: **wood goat**
Flying Star: **8**
Good day: **rabbit, pig**
Bad day: **ox**

12 sunday
Animal: **fire monkey**
Flying Star: **9**
Good day: **rat, dragon**
Bad day: **tiger**

For June, the monthly visiting inauspicious **Flying Star 7**, brings conflict, arguments, lawsuits, illness, accidents, **Robbery and Gossip**. The Flying Star 7 is much feared because of this potential of rivalry, theft, burglary, loss of wealth and violence that it can bring into one's life. It is important to be cautious during this month. It will mainly have an adverse effect on emotional and physical wellbeing especially if you are a young girls or Rooster born person. Office politics and competitions will be high. Being swindled by others is a real possibility. Watch your back during this month and be careful who you trust. Scams and trickeries are just around the corner. Be cautious if principal areas are open and in the West. Strong emotions, robbery, gossips, and villains can be averted if you steer clear of the West area.

Sickness related to the mouth and teeth may surface. There is the possibility of hospitalisation or surgery for those with existing health complications. Remedy this Star with the traditional cure of three pieces of Bamboo in a transparent glass vase of water in the Western location; the Evil Eye symbol with seven glass elephants, or place one Blue Rhinoceros and one Blue Elephant, or a pair of Blue Rhinoceros figurines in this sector, facing out of the home. A water feature also helps exhausting the metal energy of the flying star 7.

Pertaining to the Luo Shu or Bagua school of Feng Shui, the annual flying star 7 sits in the West sector for 2022, this sector is representative of descendants, family and children luck, and the protection of your current assets and wealth.

The West sector is the home of the celestial white tiger, so placing the symbolism of Tiger in the West can protect the luck of the family. Place any wealth symbolism in the West area to assist protection and for the family to stay together remaining healthy and strong. The West belongs to the element of Metal. For 2022 enhance wealth luck with Gold Coins, Gold Ingots, a Wealth God, metallic artwork, paintings or colours. The West wall is the favorable position for family photos in metallic frames.

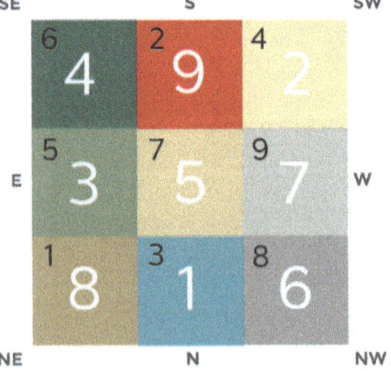

06 | 2022 June

THE WATER TIGER YEAR

13 monday
Animal: **fire rooster**
Flying Star: **1**
Good day: **ox, snake**
Bad day: **rabbit**

14 tuesday
Animal: **earth dog**
Flying Star: **2**
Good day: **tiger, horse**
Bad day: **dragon**

15 wednesday
Animal: **earth pig**
Flying Star: **3**
Good day: **rabbit, goat**
Bad day: **snake**

16 thursday
Animal: **metal rat**
Flying Star: **4**
Good day: **dragon, monkey**
Bad day: **horse**

17 friday
Animal: **metal ox**
Flying Star: **5**
Good day: **snake, rooster**
Bad day: **goat**

18 saturday
Animal: **water tiger**
Flying Star: **6**
Good day: **horse, dog**
Bad day: **monkey**

19 sunday
Animal: **water rabbit**
Flying Star: **7**
Good day: **goat, pig**
Bad day: **rooster**

Place TV and stereo equipment on the West wall for long term good fortune.

06 | 2022 June

THE WATER TIGER YEAR

20 monday

Animal: **wood dragon**
Flying Star: **8**
Good day: **rat, monkey**
Bad day: **dog**

21 tuesday

Animal: **wood snake**
Flying Star: **9/1**
Good day: **ox, rooster**
Bad day: **pig**

22 wednesday

Animal: **fire horse**
Flying Star: **9**
Good day: **tiger, dog**
Bad day: **rat**

23 thursday

Animal: **fire goat**
Flying Star: **8**
Good day: **rabbit, pig**
Bad day: **ox**

24 friday

Animal: **earth monkey**
Flying Star: **7**
Good day: **rat, dragon**
Bad day: **tiger**

25 saturday

Animal: **earth rooster**
Flying Star: **6**
Good day: **ox, snake**
Bad day: **rabbit**

26 sunday

Animal: **metal dog**
Flying Star: **5**
Good day: **tiger, horse**
Bad day: **dragon**

07 | 2022 July

THE WATER TIGER YEAR

27 monday
Animal: **metal pig**
Flying Star: **4**
Good day: **rabbit, goat**
Bad day: **snake**

28 tuesday
Animal: **water rat**
Flying Star: **3**
Good day: **dragon, monkey**
Bad day: **horse**

29 wednesday
Animal: **water ox**
Flying Star: **2**
Good day: **snake, rooster**
Bad day: **goat**

30 thursday
Animal: **wood tiger**
Flying Star: **1**
Good day: **horse, dog**
Bad day: **monkey**

1 friday
Animal: **wood rabbit**
Flying Star: **9**
Good day: **goat, pig**
Bad day: **rooster**

❤️

2 saturday
Animal: **fire dragon**
Flying Star: **8**
Good day: **rat, monkey**
Bad day: **dog**

3 sunday
Animal: **fire snake**
Flying Star: **7**
Good day: **ox, rooster**
Bad day: **pig**

JULY 2022

GOAT

(1919, 1931, 1943, 1955, 1967, 1979, 1991, 2003, 2015)

Stable, determined, hardworking, and willing. They are survivors, not a leader, but make effective team worker. They are observant, great listeners and need to have people around them. Goats like harmony but do not like to be alone.

Favourable monthly animal – Horse, Rabbit, Pig

Unfavourable monthly animal - Ox

07 | 2022 July

THE WATER TIGER YEAR

4 monday
Animal: **earth horse**
Flying Star: **6**
Good day: **tiger, dog**
Bad day: **rat**

5 tuesday
Animal: **earth goat**
Flying Star: **5**
Good day: **rabbit, pig**
Bad day: **ox**

6 wednesday
Animal: **metal monkey**
Flying Star: **4**
Good day: **rat, dragon**
Bad day: **tiger**

7 thursday
Animal: **metal rooster**
Flying Star: **3**
Good day: **ox, snake**
Bad day: **rabbit**

8 friday
Animal: **water dog**
Flying Star: **2**
Good day: **tiger, horse**
Bad day: **dragon**

9 saturday
Animal: **water pig**
Flying Star: **1**
Good day: **rabbit, goat**
Bad day: **snake**

10 sunday
Animal: **wood rat**
Flying Star: **9**
Good day: **dragon, monkey**
Bad day: **horse**

For July, there will be the monthly visiting **Flying Star 6**, a **Star bringing authority, power, wealth, speculative, windfall heaven luck** that is poised to bring good fortune, encouraging manifestation of career prospects. It is said to bring enhanced power, status, authority, good name, and prosperity luck as well as career luck straight from heaven. It is also known as an indirect wealth Star of good luck also straight from heaven that bodes well for professional activities, especially if you want to climb the career ladder or achieve higher recognition at work. The Patriarch, older men, Dog and Pig are the most likely to benefit. The authority that is brought upon by the positive aspects of this Star can also indicate status and influence in social circles.

Bring life to this Star with Yang energy such as water feature, sound, and activity. Traditional enhancers include a Horse figurine, Six Gold Coins on tassel, or Gold Ingots.

If activated by negative external forms the lucky 6 can turn abruptly and bring with its sudden upheavals, changes and medical complications to the kidney or legs.

Pertaining to the Luo Shu or Bagua school of Feng Shui, the annual flying star 6 sits in the North-West sector for 2022, this sector is representative of the man of the house, signifies influential benefactors, mentors, and helpful people.

The North West belongs to the element of Metal, in Chinese culture metal also signifies gold. So, this is also a pocket of family wealth. To tap into and enhance, use metal décor items, coloured objects, bells or windchimes. The three Star Gods, represent health, wealth and longevity and are excellent used in the main living area of a home to benefit all occupants

07 | 2022 July

THE WATER TIGER YEAR

11 monday
Animal: **wood ox**
Flying Star: **8**
Good day: **snake, rooster**
Bad day: **goat**

12 tuesday
Animal: **fire tiger**
Flying Star: **7**
Good day: **horse, dog**
Bad day: **monkey**

13 wednesday
Animal: **fire rabbit**
Flying Star: **6**
Good day: **goat, pig**
Bad day: **rooster**

14 thursday
Animal: **earth dragon**
Flying Star: **5**
Good day: **rat, monkey**
Bad day: **dog**

15 friday
Animal: **earth snake**
Flying Star: **4**
Good day: **ox, rooster**
Bad day: **pig**

16 saturday
Animal: **metal horse**
Flying Star: **3**
Good day: **tiger, dog**
Bad day: **rat**

17 sunday
Animal: **metal goat**
Flying Star: **2**
Good day: **rabbit, pig**
Bad day: **ox**

07 | 2022 July

THE WATER TIGER YEAR

18 monday
Animal: **water monkey**
Flying Star: **1**
Good day: **rat, dragon**
Bad day: **tiger**

19 tuesday
Animal: **water rooster**
Flying Star: **9**
Good day: **ox, snake**
Bad day: **rabbit**

20 wednesday
Animal: **wood dog**
Flying Star: **8**
Good day: **tiger, horse**
Bad day: **dragon**

21 thursday
Animal: **wood pig**
Flying Star: **7**
Good day: **rabbit, goat**
Bad day: **snake**

22 friday
Animal: **fire rat**
Flying Star: **6**
Good day: **dragon, monkey**
Bad day: **horse**

23 saturday
Animal: **fire ox**
Flying Star: **5**
Good day: **snake, rooster**
Bad day: **goat**

24 sunday
Animal: **earth tiger**
Flying Star: **4**
Good day: **horse, dog**
Bad day: **monkey**

Fire at Heaven's Gate. The Northwest corner of any home or room signifies Heaven. It is inauspicious to have fire in the Northwest..

07 | 2022 July

THE WATER TIGER YEAR

25 monday
Animal: **earth rabbit**
Flying Star: **3**
Good day: **goat, pig**
Bad day: **rooster**

26 tuesday
Animal: **metal dragon**
Flying Star: **2**
Good day: **rat, monkey**
Bad day: **dog**

27 wednesday
Animal: **metal snake**
Flying Star: **1**
Good day: **ox, rooster**
Bad day: **pig**

28 thursday
Animal: **water horse**
Flying Star: **9**
Good day: **tiger, dog**
Bad day: **rat**

29 friday
Animal: **water goat**
Flying Star: **8**
Good day: **rabbit, pig**
Bad day: **ox**

30 saturday
Animal: **wood monkey**
Flying Star: **7**
Good day: **rat, dragon**
Bad day: **tiger**

31 sunday
Animal: **wood rooster**
Flying Star: **6**
Good day: **ox, snake**
Bad day: **rabbit**

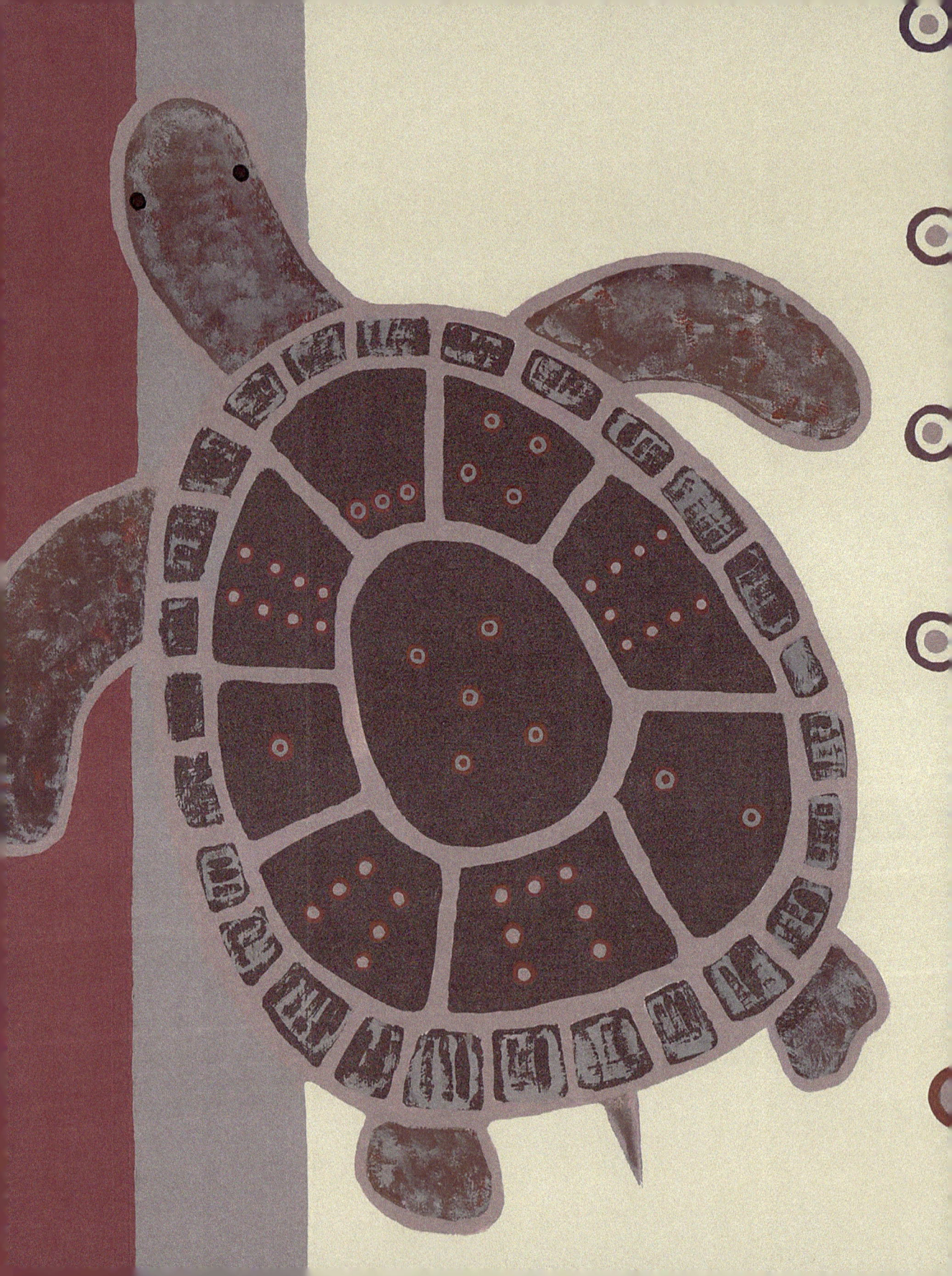

08 | 2022 August

THE WATER TIGER YEAR

1 monday
Animal: **fire dog**
Flying Star: **5**
Good day: **tiger, horse**
Bad day: **dragon**

2 tuesday
Animal: **fire pig**
Flying Star: **4**
Good day: **rabbit, goat**
Bad day: **snake**

3 wednesday
Animal: **earth rat**
Flying Star: **3**
Good day: **dragon, monkey**
Bad day: **horse**

4 thursday
Animal: **earth ox**
Flying Star: **2**
Good day: **snake, rooster**
Bad day: **goat**

5 friday
Animal: **metal tiger**
Flying Star: **1**
Good day: **horse, dog**
Bad day: **monkey**

6 saturday
Animal: **metal rabbit**
Flying Star: **9**
Good day: **goat, pig**
Bad day: **rooster**

7 sunday
Animal: **water dragon**
Flying Star: **8**
Good day: **rat, monkey**
Bad day: **dog**

AUGUST 2022

MONKEY

(1920, 1932, 1944, 1956, 1968, 1980, 1992, 2004, 2016)

Fast thinkers, very quick learners, creative, but can be insensitive. They don't bear grudges, are highly independent and make friends quickly. They are helpful, self-confident, high achievers, ambitious, competitive, and determined and very rarely give up.

Favourable monthly animal - snake, rat, dragon

Unfavourable monthly animal - tiger

08 | 2022 August

THE WATER TIGER YEAR

8 monday
Animal: **water snake**
Flying Star: **7**
Good day: **ox, rooster**
Bad day: **pig**

9 tuesday
Animal: **wood horse**
Flying Star: **6**
Good day: **tiger, dog**
Bad day: **rat**

10 wednesday
Animal: **wood goat**
Flying Star: **5**
Good day: **rabbit, pig**
Bad day: **ox**

11 thursday
Animal: **fire monkey**
Flying Star: **4**
Good day: **rat, dragon**
Bad day: **tiger**

12 friday
Animal: **fire rooster**
Flying Star: **3**
Good day: **ox, snake**
Bad day: **rabbit**

13 saturday
Animal: **earth dog**
Flying Star: **2**
Good day: **tiger, horse**
Bad day: **dragon**

14 sunday
Animal: **earth pig**
Flying Star: **1**
Good day: **rabbit, goat**
Bad day: **snake**

For August, there will be the monthly visiting **Flying Star 5** (also known as the 5 Yellow Star), the most dangerous, vicious, and aggressive of all Stars. It is the **Star of Danger, misfortune, money loss, problems, bad luck, obstacles, calamities, accidents, illness, and mishaps**. It is always very bad news. It is a malicious Star feared by all Feng Shui-wise as it has the tendency to attract unfavorable outcomes, bad luck of all kinds. This can range from loss of money or salary, that can be very serious. It has been thought to cause major disruption in business plans or even major accidents with serious injuries, which includes fatal accidents. With many damaging manifestations like bankruptcy, betrayals, disloyalty, obstacles, tragedies, mishaps, and anything else that is negative, depressing, and hazardous.

Best not to break ground or attempt new renovation projects. The most effective way to combat the 5 Star is to leave it alone to the best of your ability – do not disturb it! If that is not possible it can be pacified with a Brass Pagoda, Bonze bell, metal windchimes, along with a Saltwater Cure. You can also use a Ganesha to assist with removing of obstacles.

To counter effects of this negative star, you can place heavy Metal objects made of brass, cooper, bronze, or pewter in the Centre of your home. Metallic artwork, colours and home décor items. Reduce and remove Fire and earth energy.

Pertaining to the Luo Shu or Bagua school of Feng Shui, the annual flying star 5 sits in the Centre sector for 2022, this sector is representative of health, physical, emotional, and spiritual wellbeing.

The Centre belongs to the element of Earth. Earth generates Metal so this is a good relationship. Earth provides foundation and nourishment. The Centre of your home should be open and clear. This allows energy to flow freely and connect all areas to one another. If the energy is blocked in the Centre such as with a staircase or bathroom try to create as much grounded energy as you can with the Earth Element by using square shapes, earthy colours such as yellow and tan, or objects made from earth e.g., ceramic tiles.

08 | 2022 August

THE WATER TIGER YEAR

15 monday
Animal: **metal rat**
Flying Star: **9**
Good day: **dragon, monkey**
Bad day: **horse**

16 tuesday
Animal: **metal ox**
Flying Star: **8**
Good day: **snake, rooster**
Bad day: **goat**

17 wednesday
Animal: **water tiger**
Flying Star: **7**
Good day: **horse, dog**
Bad day: **monkey**

18 thursday
Animal: **water rabbit**
Flying Star: **6**
Good day: **goat, pig**
Bad day: **rooster**

19 friday
Animal: **wood dragon**
Flying Star: **5**
Good day: **rat, monkey**
Bad day: **dog**

20 saturday
Animal: **wood snake**
Flying Star: **4**
Good day: **ox, rooster**
Bad day: **pig**

21 sunday
Animal: **fire horse**
Flying Star: **3**
Good day: **tiger, dog**
Bad day: **rat**

Living rooms must have at least one solid wall. To allow the chi to flow and be supported.

08 | 2022 August

THE WATER TIGER YEAR

22 monday
Animal: **fire goat**
Flying Star: **2**
Good day: **rabbit, pig**
Bad day: **ox**

23 tuesday
Animal: **earth monkey**
Flying Star: **1**
Good day: **rat, dragon**
Bad day: **tiger**

24 wednesday
Animal: **earth rooster**
Flying Star: **9**
Good day: **ox, snake**
Bad day: **rabbit**

25 thursday
Animal: **metal dog**
Flying Star: **8**
Good day: **tiger, horse**
Bad day: **dragon**

26 friday
Animal: **metal pig**
Flying Star: **7**
Good day: **rabbit, goat**
Bad day: **snake**

27 saturday
Animal: **water rat**
Flying Star: **6**
Good day: **dragon, monkey**
Bad day: **horse**

28 sunday
Animal: **water ox**
Flying Star: **5**
Good day: **snake, rooster**
Bad day: **goat**

09 | 2022 September

THE WATER TIGER YEAR

29 monday

Animal: **wood tiger**
Flying Star: **4**
Good day: **horse, dog**
Bad day: **monkey**

30 tuesday

Animal: **wood rabbit**
Flying Star: **3**
Good day: **goat, pig**
Bad day: **rooster**

31 wednesday

Animal: **fire dragon**
Flying Star: **2**
Good day: **rat, monkey**
Bad day: **dog**

1 thursday

Animal: **fire snake**
Flying Star: **1**
Good day: **ox, rooster**
Bad day: **pig**

2 friday

Animal: **earth horse**
Flying Star: **9**
Good day: **tiger, dog**
Bad day: **rat**

3 saturday

Animal: **earth goat**
Flying Star: **8**
Good day: **rabbit, pig**
Bad day: **ox**

4 sunday

Animal: **metal monkey**
Flying Star: **7**
Good day: **rat, dragon**
Bad day: **tiger**

SEPTEMBER 2022

ROOSTER

(1921, 1933, 1945, 1957, 1969, 1981, 1993, 2005, 2017)

Unique energy in relationships and friendships. They are musical, creative, artistic, imaginative and inventive; can be drama queens or kings. They can be focused and persistent; know what they want, great talkers, debaters and negotiators. straight forward, honest with others; they make great friends. They are sensitive to relationships, vulnerable and they tend to bottle up their feelings. They will rarely fight back, but when they do it is with full power.

Favourable monthly animal – dragon ox snake

Unfavourable monthly animal - rabbit

09 | 2022 September

THE WATER TIGER YEAR

5 monday
Animal: **metal rooster**
Flying Star: **6**
Good day: **ox, snake**
Bad day: **rabbit**

6 tuesday
Animal: **water dog**
Flying Star: **5**
Good day: **tiger, horse**
Bad day: **dragon**

7 wednesday
Animal: **water pig**
Flying Star: **4**
Good day: **rabbit, goat**
Bad day: **snake**

8 thursday
Animal: **wood rat**
Flying Star: **3**
Good day: **dragon, monkey**
Bad day: **horse**

9 friday
Animal: **wood ox**
Flying Star: **2**
Good day: **snake, rooster**
Bad day: **goat**

10 saturday
Animal: **fire tiger**
Flying Star: **1**
Good day: **horse, dog**
Bad day: **monkey**

11 sunday
Animal: **fire rabbit**
Flying Star: **9**
Good day: **goat, pig**
Bad day: **rooster**

For September, the monthly visiting **Flying Star 4** brings **romance intelligence, talent, wisdom, fame, promotion, academic, scholastic and literacy luck** to all. It is also often called the Peach Blossom Star or a Star of beauty, knowledge, and learning. In 2022, it stands to affect mostly those born in the year of the Dragon and Snake, as well eldest daughters. Generally, this Star brings about harmony and happiness in love relationships. It is highly auspicious for singles that are searching for love and marriage. Bringing about meaningful and fulfilling relationships. Those with a literary, artistic, or creative background such as lecturers, teachers, artists, writers, and researchers will see positive results in their work, with indication of further advancement. Students this month will have better examination luck and better luck in applications for admission to good schools or Universities.

To maintain and enhance love and romance in relationships, couples should strongly consider placing two Rose Quartz crystals next to or under their bed. You can also display love symbols such as Mandarin Ducks, Wish fulfilling birds or Huggers. To enhance Academic luck, display Chinese ink brush / artwork, tiered pagoda, the Chinese saint Luohan or three Star Gods.

Pertaining to the Luo Shu or Bagua school of Feng Shui, the annual flying star 4 sits in the South-East sector for 2022, this sector is representative and governed by wealth and prosperity, income, cashflow and earnings.

The Southeast belongs to the element of Wood, to tap into money luck enhance this area with a water picture or water feature, water strengthens the wood energy, flowers, plants, green colours and water tones will also help strength the luck. Always make sure the water flow is entering the home and not leaving ...

09 | 2022 September

THE WATER TIGER YEAR

12 monday
Animal: **earth dragon**
Flying Star: **8**
Good day: **rat, monkey**
Bad day: **dog**

13 tuesday
Animal: **earth snake**
Flying Star: **7**
Good day: **ox, rooster**
Bad day: **pig**

14 wednesday
Animal: **metal horse**
Flying Star: **6**
Good day: **tiger, dog**
Bad day: **rat**

15 thursday
Animal: **metal goat**
Flying Star: **5**
Good day: **rabbit, pig**
Bad day: **ox**

16 friday
Animal: **water monkey**
Flying Star: **4**
Good day: **rat, dragon**
Bad day: **tiger**

17 saturday
Animal: **water rooster**
Flying Star: **3**
Good day: **ox, snake**
Bad day: **rabbit**

18 sunday
Animal: **wood dog**
Flying Star: **2**
Good day: **tiger, horse**
Bad day: **dragon**

Grow Oranges, Cumquats and Limes. Weighed down heavenly with ripened fruit symbolizes prosperity.

09 | 2022 September

THE WATER TIGER YEAR

19 monday
Animal: **wood pig**
Flying Star: **1**
Good day: **rabbit, goat**
Bad day: **snake**

20 tuesday
Animal: **fire rat**
Flying Star: **9**
Good day: **dragon, monkey**
Bad day: **horse**

21 wednesday
Animal: **fire ox**
Flying Star: **8**
Good day: **snake, rooster**
Bad day: **goat**

22 thursday
Animal: **earth tiger**
Flying Star: **7**
Good day: **horse, dog**
Bad day: **monkey**

23 friday
Animal: **earth rabbit**
Flying Star: **6**
Good day: **goat, pig**
Bad day: **rooster**

24 saturday
Animal: **metal dragon**
Flying Star: **5**
Good day: **rat, monkey**
Bad day: **dog**

25 sunday
Animal: **metal snake**
Flying Star: **4**
Good day: **ox, rooster**
Bad day: **pig**

ACTIVATING PEACH BLOSSOM LUCK

Feng Shui can prescribe a simple formula for helping singles who are looking for love and romance - it is as easy as activating your 'Peach Blossom Luck.'

If you are a TIGER, HORSE or DOG place a Rabbit in the East of your bedroom.

If you are an OX, SNAKE or ROOSET place a Horse in the South of your bedroom.

If you are a RAT, DRAGON or MONKEY place a Rooster in the West of your bedroom.

If you are a RABBIT, GOAT or PIG place a Rat in the North of your bedroom.

09 | 2022 September

THE WATER TIGER YEAR

26 monday
Animal: **water horse**
Flying Star: **3**
Good day: **tiger, dog**
Bad day: **rat**

27 tuesday
Animal: **water goat**
Flying Star: **2**
Good day: **rabbit, pig**
Bad day: **ox**

28 wednesday
Animal: **wood monkey**
Flying Star: **1**
Good day: **rat, dragon**
Bad day: **tiger**

29 thursday
Animal: **wood rooster**
Flying Star: **9**
Good day: **ox, snake**
Bad day: **rabbit**

30 friday
Animal: **fire dog**
Flying Star: **8**
Good day: **tiger, horse**
Bad day: **dragon**

1 saturday
Animal: **fire pig**
Flying Star: **7**
Good day: **rabbit, goat**
Bad day: **snake**

2 sunday
Animal: **earth rat**
Flying Star: **6**
Good day: **dragon, monkey**
Bad day: **horse**

10

2022 October

THE WATER TIGER YEAR

3 monday

Animal: **earth ox**
Flying Star: **5**
Good day: **snake, rooster**
Bad day: **goat**

4 tuesday

Animal: **metal tiger**
Flying Star: **4**
Good day: **horse, dog**
Bad day: **monkey**

❤️

5 wednesday

Animal: **metal rabbit**
Flying Star: **3**
Good day: **goat, pig**
Bad day: **rooster**

6 thursday

Animal: **water dragon**
Flying Star: **2**
Good day: **rat, monkey**
Bad day: **dog**

7 friday

Animal: **water snake**
Flying Star: **1**
Good day: **ox, rooster**
Bad day: **pig**

✒️✂️🚜

8 saturday

Animal: **wood horse**
Flying Star: **9**
Good day: **tiger, dog**
Bad day: **rat**

9 sunday

Animal: **wood goat**
Flying Star: **8**
Good day: **rabbit, pig**
Bad day: **ox**

OCTOBER 2022

DOG

(1922, 1934, 1946, 1958, 1970, 1982, 1994, 2006, 2018)

Ready for action, energetic, gains respect, brave but they take risks. They are helpful, loyal, reliable, determined, competent and confident. Dogs will not let go of ideas and ambitions and are likely to see things to the end. They are caring and a great listener. They are very efficient and make great workers, but they are not leaders.

Favourable monthly animal – rabbit, tiger, horse

Unfavourable monthly animal - dragon

10 | 2022 October

THE WATER TIGER YEAR

10 monday
Animal: **fire monkey**
Flying Star: **7**
Good day: **rat, dragon**
Bad day: **tiger**

11 tuesday
Animal: **fire rooster**
Flying Star: **6**
Good day: **ox, snake**
Bad day: **rabbit**

12 wednesday
Animal: **earth dog**
Flying Star: **5**
Good day: **tiger, horse**
Bad day: **dragon**

13 thursday
Animal: **earth pig**
Flying Star: **4**
Good day: **rabbit, goat**
Bad day: **snake**

14 friday
Animal: **metal rat**
Flying Star: **3**
Good day: **dragon, monkey**
Bad day: **horse**

15 saturday
Animal: **metal ox**
Flying Star: **2**
Good day: **snake, rooster**
Bad day: **goat**

16 sunday
Animal: **water tiger**
Flying Star: **1**
Good day: **horse, dog**
Bad day: **monkey**

For October, the monthly visiting **Flying Star 3** brings **gossip, arguments, legal trouble, conflict, and disputes**. It is a hostile Star, known for bringing about violence, anger, misunderstandings, constant disagreements, heated arguments, litigation, trouble with authorities and in extreme cases, legal complications between family members, friends and or colleagues.

Health issues related to the liver, gall bladder, feet and arms may arise. As the yearly flying star sits in the East and the East belongs to the wood element. Relationships between spouses will be affected with high tension energies. Harmony of families and stability of marriages will be affected. Watch out for trouble with the authorities or you may be hit with litigation. Eldest sons, and Rabbits are the most likely to be affected.

Cures to be placed for October include a red piece of paper which is the traditional Chinese cure, or other red and purple décor objects, candles, or bright lights. A Magic Flaming Wheel can also be used. The red phoenix or the image of an eagle. If your front door is in the East sector, it would benefit you greatly by placing Temple Lions there for extra protection along with an Evil Eye Symbol.

Pertaining to the Luo Shu or Bagua school of Feng Shui, the annual flying star 3 sits in the East sector for 2022, this sector is representative of good health and longevity.

The East belongs to the element of Wood, enhance for positive health and wellbeing by strengthen with water and wood therefore lucky bamboo in water is such a powerful cure. Greenery, plants, and flowers are also acceptable to strengthen the sector. The east sector is the home of the celestial green dragon, so placing the symbolism of dragon in the East can maximise the luck of the family. A Quan Yin can also be used to safeguard health and wellbeing.

10 | 2022 October

THE WATER TIGER YEAR

17 monday

Animal: **water rabbit**
Flying Star: **9**
Good day: **goat, pig**
Bad day: **rooster**

18 tuesday

Animal: **wood dragon**
Flying Star: **8**
Good day: **rat, monkey**
Bad day: **dog**

19 wednesday

Animal: **wood snake**
Flying Star: **7**
Good day: **ox, rooster**
Bad day: **pig**

20 thursday

Animal: **fire horse**
Flying Star: **6**
Good day: **tiger, dog**
Bad day: **rat**

21 friday

Animal: **fire goat**
Flying Star: **5**
Good day: **rabbit, pig**
Bad day: **ox**

22 saturday

Animal: **earth monkey**
Flying Star: **4**
Good day: **rat, dragon**
Bad day: **tiger**

23 sunday

Animal: **earth rooster**
Flying Star: **3**
Good day: **ox, snake**
Bad day: **rabbit**

Why a round table? From a feng shui point of view it is said a round or oval table is considered better than a rectangle or square table. As being rounded, the shape is flowing, contributing to a mor even distribution and flow of energy ...

10 | 2022 October

THE WATER TIGER YEAR

24 monday

Animal: **metal dog**
Flying Star: **2**
Good day: **tiger, horse**
Bad day: **dragon**

25 tuesday

Animal: **metal pig**
Flying Star: **1**
Good day: **rabbit, goat**
Bad day: **snake**

26 wednesday

Animal: **water rat**
Flying Star: **9**
Good day: **dragon, monkey**
Bad day: **horse**

27 thursday

Animal: **water ox**
Flying Star: **8**
Good day: **snake, rooster**
Bad day: **goat**

28 friday

Animal: **wood tiger**
Flying Star: **7**
Good day: **horse, dog**
Bad day: **monkey**

29 saturday

Animal: **wood rabbit**
Flying Star: **6**
Good day: **rabbit, pig**
Bad day: **rooster**

30 sunday

Animal: **fire dragon**
Flying Star: **5**
Good day: **rat, monkey**
Bad day: **dog**

11

2022
November

THE WATER TIGER YEAR

31 monday

Animal: **fire snake**
Flying Star: **4**
Good day: **ox, rooster**
Bad day: **pig**

1 tuesday

Animal: **earth horse**
Flying Star: **3**
Good day: **tiger, dog**
Bad day: **rat**

2 wednesday

Animal: **earth goat**
Flying Star: **2**
Good day: **rabbit, pig**
Bad day: **ox**

3 thursday

Animal: **metal monkey**
Flying Star: **1**
Good day: **rat, dragon**
Bad day: **tiger**

4 friday

Animal: **metal rooster**
Flying Star: **9**
Good day: **ox, snake**
Bad day: **rabbit**

5 saturday

Animal: **water dog**
Flying Star: **8**
Good day: **tiger, horse**
Bad day: **dragon**

6 sunday

Animal: **water pig**
Flying Star: **7**
Good day: **rabbit, goat**
Bad day: **snake**

NOVEMBER 2022

PIG

(1923, 1935, 1947, 1959, 1971, 1983 1995, 2007, 2019)

Energy of Wealth in many forms has a sense of time, not in a hurry, can be sluggish and not ambitious. Not very intellectually competitive and has natural humility. They accumulate and are usually rotund. They are accepting, intelligent, perceptive, and independent and can be considerably determined. They are also reliable and wise in times of a crisis.

Favourable monthly animal - Tiger, Rabbit, Goat

Unfavourable monthly animal - Snake

11

2022
November

THE WATER TIGER YEAR

7
monday

Animal: **wood rat**
Flying Star: **6**
Good day: **dragon, monkey**
Bad day: **horse**

8
tuesday

Animal: **wood ox**
Flying Star: **5**
Good day: **snake, rooster**
Bad day: **goat**

9
wednesday

Animal: **fire tiger**
Flying Star: **4**
Good day: **horse, dog**
Bad day: **monkey**

10
thursday

Animal: **fire rabbit**
Flying Star: **3**
Good day: **goat, pig**
Bad day: **rooster**

11
friday

Animal: **earth dragon**
Flying Star: **2**
Good day: **rat, monkey**
Bad day: **dog**

12
saturday

Animal: **earth snake**
Flying Star: **1**
Good day: **ox, rooster**
Bad day: **pig**

13
sunday

Animal: **metal horse**
Flying Star: **9**
Good day: **tiger, dog**
Bad day: **rat**

For November, the monthly visiting **Flying Star 2** brings **turbulent energies, negative people, illness, sickness, disease and stress** to all homes and businesses.

It is an Earth element Star that threatens to bring turbulent energies wreaking havoc on health, illness, disease, and those with existing or persistent health problems. It is believed to worsen an existing illness. In 2022, the matriarch, elderly and pregnant women will be affected by this negative Star the most. In 2022, it will affect you if your front door is in the Southwest, main bedroom or living area; or Monkey and Goat born people, will experience feeling physically and mentally weak. The flying star 2 has the potential to bring positive property related or real estate investments but it will come at the cost of health.

It is strongly advised to help cure the Southwest of your home and business with a Health Gourd, (also known as a Wu Lou), Six Gold Coins on red tassel, a Saltwater Cure, and a Quan Yin. If possible, wear a Wu Lou pendant or carry a Wu Lou amulet if you are a Monkey or a Goat. Metal bell or windchime, can be used but the Metal energy is to be reasonably still and heavy, so metal wall sculptures work better instead.

To counter effects of this negative star, you can place heavy Metal objects made of brass, cooper, bronze, or pewter in this sector. Metallic artwork, colours, white, silver, gold, and home décor items. Reduce and remove Fire and earth energy

Pertaining to the Luo Shu or Bagua school of Feng Shui, the annual flying star 2 sits in the Southwest sector for 2022 this sector is representative of relationship luck, love, romance, and marriage.

The Southwest belongs to the element of earth, to enhance the Southwest of your home for positive relationship luck, use earth and fire energy to support, amethyst, rose quartz crystal, purple, pink, red peonies, double happiness symbol, a pair of Mandarin Ducks, symbolism of couples and bright lights is recommended in this sector.

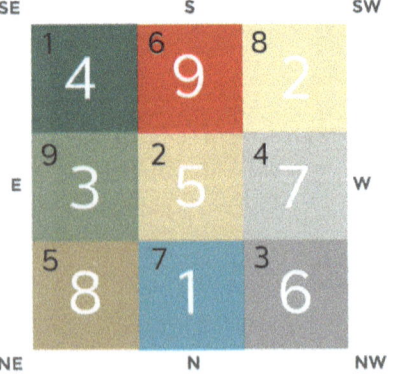

11

2022
November

THE WATER TIGER YEAR

14
monday

Animal: **metal goat**
Flying Star: **8**
Good day: **rabbit, pig**
Bad day: **ox**

15
tuesday

Animal: **water monkey**
Flying Star: **7**
Good day: **rat, dragon**
Bad day: **tiger**

16
wednesday

Animal: **water rooster**
Flying Star: **6**
Good day: **ox, snake**
Bad day: **rabbit**

17
thursday

Animal: **wood dog**
Flying Star: **5**
Good day: **tiger, horse**
Bad day: **dragon**

18
friday

Animal: **wood pig**
Flying Star: **4**
Good day: **rabbit, goat**
Bad day: **snake**

19
saturday

Animal: **fire rat**
Flying Star: **3**
Good day: **dragon, monkey**
Bad day: **horse**

20
sunday

Animal: **fire ox**
Flying Star: **2**
Good day: **snake, rooster**
Bad day: **goat**

Crystals best in the Southwest especially rose quartz for love and opening heart chakra ... Southwest sector relates to people love and relationship luck and is the best sector for crystals. Love and relationship luck is such an essential part of getting your feng shui right and in balance ... happy love and people luck, is corner stone of better health and wealth...

11

2022
November

THE WATER TIGER YEAR

21 monday

Animal: **earth tiger**
Flying Star: **1**
Good day: **horse, dog**
Bad day: **monkey**

22 tuesday

Animal: **earth rabbit**
Flying Star: **9**
Good day: **goat, pig**
Bad day: **rooster**

23 wednesday

Animal: **metal dragon**
Flying Star: **8**
Good day: **rat, monkey**
Bad day: **dog**

24 thursday

Animal: **metal snake**
Flying Star: **7**
Good day: **ox, rooster**
Bad day: **pig**

25 friday

Animal: **water horse**
Flying Star: **6**
Good day: **tiger, dog**
Bad day: **rat**

26 saturday

Animal: **water goat**
Flying Star: **5**
Good day: **rabbit, pig**
Bad day: **ox**

27 sunday

Animal: **wood monkey**
Flying Star: **4**
Good day: **rat, dragon**
Bad day: **tiger**

12

2022
December

THE WATER TIGER YEAR

28
monday

Animal: **wood rooster**
Flying Star: **3**
Good day: **ox, snake**
Bad day: **rabbit**

29
tuesday

Animal: **fire dog**
Flying Star: **2**
Good day: **tiger, horse**
Bad day: **dragon**

30
wednesday

Animal: **fire pig**
Flying Star: **1**
Good day: **rabbit, goat**
Bad day: **snake**

1
thursday

Animal: **earth rat**
Flying Star: **9**
Good day: **dragon, monkey**
Bad day: **horse**

2
friday

Animal: **earth ox**
Flying Star: **8**
Good day: **snake, rooster**
Bad day: **goat**

3
saturday

Animal: **metal tiger**
Flying Star: **7**
Good day: **horse, dog**
Bad day: **monkey**

4
sunday

Animal: **metal rabbit**
Flying Star: **6**
Good day: **goat, pig**
Bad day: **rooster**

DECEMBER 2022

RAT

(1924, 1936, 1948, 1960, 1972, 1984, 1996, 2008, 2020)

Enduring, persistent, adaptable, accepting, brave, curious and forgiving. Can talk too freely and can be accused of gossiping. They are fast, determined, they don't stay put and have many changes and moves in all areas of their lives; they are excited by new things.

Favourable monthly animal - Ox, Dragon, Monkey

Unfavourable monthly animal - Horse

12

2022
December

THE WATER TIGER YEAR

5
monday

Animal: **water dragon**
Flying Star: **5**
Good day: **rat, monkey**
Bad day: **dog**

6
tuesday

Animal: **water snake**
Flying Star: **4**
Good day: **ox, rooster**
Bad day: **pig**

7
wednesday

Animal: **wood horse**
Flying Star: **3**
Good day: **tiger, dog**
Bad day: **rat**

8
thursday

Animal: **wood goat**
Flying Star: **2**
Good day: **rabbit, pig**
Bad day: **ox**

9
friday

Animal: **fire monkey**
Flying Star: **1**
Good day: **rat, dragon**
Bad day: **tiger**

10
saturday

Animal: **fire rooster**
Flying Star: **9**
Good day: **ox, snake**
Bad day: **rabbit**

11
sunday

Animal: **earth dog**
Flying Star: **8**
Good day: **tiger, horse**
Bad day: **dragon**

For December, the monthly visiting **Flying Star 1**, known as the **Star of Triumph, fame, wealth, intelligence, and Success**, brings positive energies. This lucky Star is associated with winning attaining success, reputation, good name, status, and fame. It brings excellent triumphant, victory over competition, career, and academic pursuits such as writing / research and scholastic success. This lucky star derives remarkable success for wealth opportunities, networking and social circles promoting reputation with influence and victory. This month will effectively enhance noble pursuits, as well as wealth or career related pursuits especially if you are a middle son or Rat born person. Those who enjoy these good influences will be inclined to experience competitive activities.

The Flying Star 1 has a positive influence in attracting victory over past malaise and niggling health concerns. But it is wise to watch out for emotional turbulences such as emotional instability and depression can occur. The Water element brings triumph via Yang energy to this auspicious Star, which you can activate by placing metal objects, windchime your collection of trophies and medals. water feature, a Victory Horse figurine and a Ruyi in this sector.

Pertaining to the Luo Shu or Bagua school of Feng Shui, the annual flying star 1 sits in the North sector for 2022 this sector is representative of career and business luck.

The North belongs to the element of Water, to enhance the North of your home for career and business support and luck place metal colours like white, silver, gold, pewter, bronze and black to support the water energy, metal decor objects, blue black tones or water pictures and décor items. A Black Tortoise or Dragon Tortoise.

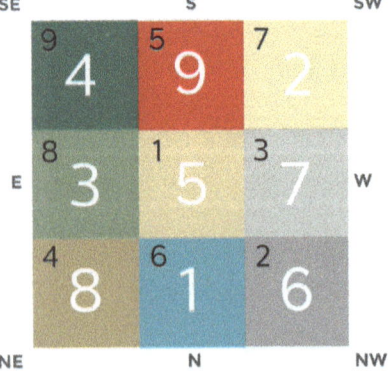

12 | 2022 December

THE WATER TIGER YEAR

12 monday
Animal: **earth pig**
Flying Star: **7**
Good day: **rabbit, goat**
Bad day: **snake**

13 tuesday
Animal: **metal rat**
Flying Star: **6**
Good day: **dragon, monkey**
Bad day: **horse**

14 wednesday
Animal: **metal ox**
Flying Star: **5**
Good day: **snake, rooster**
Bad day: **goat**

15 thursday
Animal: **water tiger**
Flying Star: **4**
Good day: **horse, dog**
Bad day: **monkey**

16 friday
Animal: **water rabbit**
Flying Star: **3**
Good day: **goat, pig**
Bad day: **rooster**

17 saturday
Animal: **wood dragon**
Flying Star: **2**
Good day: **rat, monkey**
Bad day: **dog**

18 sunday
Animal: **wood snake**
Flying Star: **1**
Good day: **ox, rooster**
Bad day: **pig**

Water should always flow in and towards home, business, or building... Feng Shui... lucky bamboo plant for longevity and health. Place 3 single stems of bamboo in a vase of water with glass pebbles and fill vase to top with water. Best in the East for health and longevity, the Southeast for money luck and in the West of the home or building in 2022 for protection.

12

2022 December

THE WATER TIGER YEAR

19 monday
Animal: **fire horse**
Flying Star: **9**
Good day: **tiger, dog**
Bad day: **rat**

20 tuesday
Animal: **fire goat**
Flying Star: **8**
Good day: **rabbit, pig**
Bad day: **ox**

21 wednesday
Animal: **earth monkey**
Flying Star: **7**
Good day: **rat, dragon**
Bad day: **tiger**

22 thursday
Animal: **earth rooster**
Flying Star: **6/4**
Good day: **ox, snake**
Bad day: **rabbit**

23 friday
Animal: **metal dog**
Flying Star: **5**
Good day: **tiger, horse**
Bad day: **dragon**

24 saturday
Animal: **metal pig**
Flying Star: **6**
Good day: **rabbit, goat**
Bad day: **snake**

25 sunday
Animal: **water rat**
Flying Star: **7**
Good day: **dragon, monkey**
Bad day: **horse**

GOOD AND BAD DAYS BASED ON ANIMAL SIGNS

Every animal has an excellent day, a vitality day and an obstacle day. They are derived from the influence of the planets. Let's take a closer look at their meanings and what the days are for each animal.

Excellent day: Your animal's excellent day is a good day for starting new projects and celebrating happy occasions. It's a good day for you to get married, start a new job or a study program, renewing contracts such as a house lease or work contract, and planting seeds. Your spiritual energy will be at its highest on this day which makes it a good day for mediation.

Vitality day: Your animal's vitality day is a good day to undertake projects requiring an elevated level of concentration and energy. It's a day to recharge your batteries and perform uplifting activities such as shopping, going for facial or lunch with friends. It you were born on either your vitality or excellent day, you'll lead a lucky life.

Obstacle day: Your animal's obstacle day brings blockages. It's a day to avoid doing anything important. Avoid starting anything new or holding an event on this day, especially a major celebration. It's best to lay low on your obstacle day and spend it reading or doing light home duties.

Animal sign	Excellent day	Vitality day	Obstacle day
Rat	Wednesday	Tuesday	Saturday
Ox	Saturday	Wednesday	Thursday
Tiger	Thursday	Saturday	Friday
Rabbit	Thursday	Saturday	Friday
Dragon	Sunday	Wednesday	Thursday
Snake	Tuesday	Friday	Wednesday
Horse	Tuesday	Friday	Wednesday
Goat	Friday	Wednesday	Thursday
Monkey	Friday	Thursday	Tuesday
Rooster	Friday	Thursday	Tuesday
Dog	Monday	Wednesday	Thursday

12 2022 December

THE WATER TIGER YEAR

26 monday
Animal: **water ox**
Flying Star: **8**
Good day: **snake, rooster**
Bad day: **goat**

27 tuesday
Animal: **wood tiger**
Flying Star: **9**
Good day: **horse, dog**
Bad day: **monkey**

28 wednesday
Animal: **wood rabbit**
Flying Star: **1**
Good day: **goat, pig**
Bad day: **rooster**

29 thursday
Animal: **fire dragon**
Flying Star: **2**
Good day: **rat, monkey**
Bad day: **dog**

30 friday
Animal: **fire snake**
Flying Star: **3**
Good day: **ox, rooster**
Bad day: **pig**

31 saturday
Animal: **earth horse**
Flying Star: **4**
Good day: **tiger, dog**
Bad day: **rat**

1 sunday
Animal: **goat**
Flying Star: **5**
Good day: **rabbit pig**
Bad day: **ox**

2023 CALENDAR

January

Mo	Tu	We	Th	Fr	Sa	Su
						1
2	3	4	5	6	7	8
9	10	11	12	13	14	15
16	17	18	19	20	21	22
23	24	25	26	27	28	29
30	31					

February

Mo	Tu	We	Th	Fr	Sa	Su
		1	2	3	4	5
6	7	8	9	10	11	12
13	14	15	16	17	18	19
20	21	22	23	24	25	26
27	28					

March

Mo	Tu	We	Th	Fr	Sa	Su
		1	2	3	4	5
6	7	8	9	10	11	12
13	14	15	16	17	18	19
20	21	22	23	24	25	26
27	28	29	30	31		

April

Mo	Tu	We	Th	Fr	Sa	Su
					1	2
3	4	5	6	7	8	9
10	11	12	13	14	15	16
17	18	19	20	21	22	23
24	25	26	27	28	29	30

May

Mo	Tu	We	Th	Fr	Sa	Su
1	2	3	4	5	6	7
8	9	10	11	12	13	14
15	16	17	18	19	20	21
22	23	24	25	26	27	28
29	30	31				

June

Mo	Tu	We	Th	Fr	Sa	Su
			1	2	3	4
5	6	7	8	9	10	11
12	13	14	15	16	17	18
19	20	21	22	23	24	25
26	27	28	29	30		

2023 CALENDAR

July

Mo	Tu	We	Th	Fr	Sa	Su
					1	2
3	4	5	6	7	8	9
10	11	12	13	14	15	16
17	18	19	20	21	22	23
24	25	26	27	28	29	30
31						

August

Mo	Tu	We	Th	Fr	Sa	Su
	1	2	3	4	5	6
7	8	9	10	11	12	13
14	15	16	17	18	19	20
21	22	23	24	25	26	27
28	29	30	31			

September

Mo	Tu	We	Th	Fr	Sa	Su
				1	2	3
4	5	6	7	8	9	10
11	12	13	14	15	16	17
18	19	20	21	22	23	24
25	26	27	28	29	30	

October

Mo	Tu	We	Th	Fr	Sa	Su
						1
2	3	4	5	6	7	8
9	10	11	12	13	14	15
16	17	18	19	20	21	22
23	24	25	26	27	28	29
30	31					

November

Mo	Tu	We	Th	Fr	Sa	Su
		1	2	3	4	5
6	7	8	9	10	11	12
13	14	15	16	17	18	19
20	21	22	23	24	25	26
27	28	29	30			

December

Mo	Tu	We	Th	Fr	Sa	Su
				1	2	3
4	5	6	7	8	9	10
11	12	13	14	15	16	17
18	19	20	21	22	23	24
25	26	27	28	29	30	31

BEGINNERS FENG SHUI 'EASY TIPS TO ENHANCE EVERYDAY LIVING'

A beginner's guide to learning the fundamentals of Feng Shui and energy flow in the home, known as Chi. This ancient art of placement which brings balance, helps to improve the harmony and prosperity within your space. Ideal as a gift for the novice wanting to learn more or beautiful coffee table book to inspire you on your next home renovation.

Buy Beginners Feng Shui **www.completefengshui.com**

Ebook Beginners Feng Shui **www.completefengshui.com**

COMPLETE FENG SHUI NEWS IS FOR YOU - TO NAVIGATE AND UNDERSTAND YOURSELF AND ENVIRONMENT:
Monthly Subscription

- Monthly Feng Shui and Flying Star Outlook
- All 12 Animals Chinese Horoscope Forecasts and Day Masters
- Calendar Auspicious date selection... And much, much more
- Over 40 pages to navigate monthly Feng Shui

Subscribe **www.completefengshui.com**

COURSES / WORKSHOPS

2022 Year of Water Tiger Astrology & Feng Shui
2022 Complete Lifestyle Retreat
Understanding Feng Shui and your home
Landform and Symbolism... making the most of your home and interior
Show Me the Money - Chinese Astrology for Career, Wealth and Success
Lifestyle Feng Shui - Better Living with Feng Shui - Learn Compass School
Good Feng Shui... property and Real Estate
Getting to Know YOU, Beginners Chinese Astrology Part 1 & 2
Module 1 : Health, Wealth & Prosperity
Module 2: Four Pillars of Destiny Part 1 & 2
Module 3: Flying Stars Part 1 & 2
Module 4: Practitioners Course and Business Practices for a Feng Shui Business
Feng Shui Refresher workshop
Feng Shui as a Business and Career

www.completefengshui.com

info@completefengshui.com.au

MB 0421 116 799

What's App 0421 116 799

TRANSFORM AND EMPOWER YOUR LIFE WITH ABUNDANCE AND SYNCHRONICITY CONNECT MIND, BODY AND WELL BEING 2022 RETREAT

Captivate self-growth through unique experiences guaranteed to generate imprinted memories. It is time to reward yourself! Unwind and transform with this well-deserved getaway. Would you like to make a real shift, find peace, open your heart, and come alive?

Feng Shui Mind Body Wellbeing a transformational retreat completed for you!

Immerse yourself in 4 days of fun, creativity, indulgence,

Feng Shui and Chinese Astrology for connectivity of your home, mind body and spirit.

Tap into you and your home's greatest potential...

Empower your life through Feng Shui and your home. Teachings from highly regarded Feng Shui Master Michele Castle. Allow the stress to melt away on this transformational journey. Michele is one of Perth's top award-winning Feng Shui masters with over 20 years' experience and lecturer at Curtin University Perth WA.

- Attract more clarity, abundance, and direction.
- Generate a supportive nurturing environment.
- Activate your life and environment with tools for long-term sustainable results.
- Experience practical teaching firsthand through Michele's skilful abilities to shift, shave and impact your life with knowledge for yourself and home.

Have YOU been searching for a better way to live and are ready to feel more alive, to be the best 'you' that you can be? NOW is the time to activate abundance and heighten your vibration.

Last retreats experience by one lovely attendee *"What an amazing week away to unwind and relax in the beautiful setting of Wilyabrup Vineyard Estate! The 2 houses were so modern, beautifully furnished, and spacious. We each had our own private room to rest and relax in. We were lead on a very informative and interesting Chinese Astrology & Feng Shui journey throughout the week with the super talented and knowledgeable Michele Castle. Explored meditation and mind activation with the ever so calming and soothing Odette Linton.*

Spoilt with massage and mind opening breathwork with the beautiful Sylvie Martin

and experienced a fun and exciting journaling and art workshop with Kez Wickham St George where we created our own paint pour/press artworks to take home! Plus, we even had our own private tarot card reading!

The meals prepared by Michele were delicious and certainly kept us full and ready for each day! The whole retreat was relaxed and not rushed, we took each day as it came with no pressing schedules to ensure we all felt like we were on holiday, all while achieving everything planned for the week! The fact that everything was on site and we did not have to leave the estate was great too!

5-star experience from me! Thankyou Michele for planning such a wonderful retreat!"

The perfect transformation WELLNESS AND HEALING experience for self and physical wellbeing. Incredible teaching, healing, delicious food & time relaxing by the lake... Set this time aside for the small pleasures in life: relaxation, a good sleep, wonderful culinary discoveries, and ultimately discovering YOU ...

Check out https://www.facebook.com/completelifestyleretreats to view previous retreats.

ABOUT THE AUTHOR

Michele Castle has been a Feng Shui practitioner - consultant for more 2 decades. Trained by Master Raymond Lo, of Hong Kong at the Feng Shui Centre in Perth, Western Australia she has also studied with Dato Joey Yap and Lillian Too. Michele studies each year under various master's and is continually expanding her Feng Shui knowledge.

Michele taught Feng Shui, Chinese Astrology and Metaphysical studies for Asian studies unit at Curtin University.

Previously studying architectural drafting and interior design and working with interiors and renovations, on her own homes it was a natural progression to incorporate Feng Shui and metaphysical studies in her renovations. Applauded for her style, she was asked if she could do what she had been doing with her own homes to others. So, having a passion and dedication after further studies her first Feng Shui business, *Energise Life Feng Shui*, began, growing quickly and incorporating workshops, seminars and teaching it soon became known as *Complete Feng Shui*.

Michele conducts on-site Feng Shui consultations for residential and corporate clients, and as well as being an accredited teacher of Feng Shui, Michele is an author and public speaker. Michele works with residential homes, small to medium family businesses, larger corporations, developers, architects, interior designers, real estate agents, restaurants, cafes, day spas and retail stores. Michele specialises in one-on-one Chinese astrology and life path readings regarding health, love, and career opportunities.

For a business client, Michele can help with staff recruitment, assist with selecting the best location and orientation for business premises, improve the atmosphere and working environments and advise on business stationery such as letterheads and business cards.

For the residential client, Michele advises on how to improve health and harmony in the home, how to choose the best home as well as improve the chances of selling your present home, assist with identifying strengths in choosing suitable careers for the younger members of the family, guide older family members looking for a change in their current career path and how to alleviate difficulties children may be having with sleeping, studying and behaviour in general.

Michele is often in demand for speaking at events, local radio, interviewed on *Today Tonight, Better Life TV*, and is a regular on the WA television show *The Couch*, where she talks about all things Feng Shui. Michele has been recognised with local awards a winner of a Nifnex Influential 100 Awards, the New Emerging Business Award, Entrepreneur Award as well as Networking Award from the Soulful Awards Self Discovery Network on 2 occasions.

Michele teaches Feng Shui courses and workshops from beginners to practitioners alike, as well offering Feng Shui Retreats in Bali and now in WA where you can immerse yourself in 5 days of Feng Shui and Chinese Astrology; one of the world's most ancient arts and science of placement, to bring about balance between people and their environment. Michele also conducts on-site learning exercises at homes and for businesses, within Australia and overseas.

For those who have mastered the basics of Feng Shui and wish to continue their studies and share their knowledge with others, there are courses in 'Feng Shui as a Business', and the 'practitioners' course' where with practice and the correct training, one can learn to be a practitioner once mastering Feng Shui becoming an consultant. Once qualified, you have a responsibility to share the correct knowledge with your client. Choosing a Feng Shui consultant is like choosing a health care professional; you want someone who knows what they are doing, who understands your needs, and gives a reliable, knowledgeable advice.

Michele truly believes.

" Life is what our thoughts environment and energy make it".

"Change your environment and thoughts, change your life".

With the knowledge of Feng Shui, it can work to increase wealth, enhance health, and harmonise relationships.

TESTIMONALS

I have been following Michelle's Feng Shui advice for over 12 years She is an amazing, very professional person with many of her predications being very accurate. **Dot O'Sullivan**

"Michele has a wealth of knowledge of all aspects of feng shui, which she shares with generosity and clarity. She interprets the Chinese astrology charts of each member of the household with great insight and intuitive understanding. Michele is always empathetic to the needs and circumstances of her clients and has helped me and my family tremendously over the many years we have made use of her services. I highly recommend Michele and her work!" **Annie Vorster**

Michele is a True Master of Feng Shui. I have had her involved with my own homes and my workplace's for about 16 or 17 years now.

She is a pleasure to work with and knows so much about Feng Shui, and how to remedy all situations.

Having Feng Shui in my life has helped the energy of my family and workplace, and make them amazing places to want to be, you can feel the calmness and the energy flowing. I am hooked, I love the beginning of every new year, so see what is changed, I love the Bazi Charts you get too, So many interesting things about life and yourself. **Ann Meney**

Great experience with Michele. Very approachable, polite, and friendly. Michele has a lot of Feng Shui knowledge. I feel that I can still ask her questions even after she has completed my consultation and report. Will continue with Michele for all future Feng Shui and interior design matters. **Mary Valentina**

We have been knowing Michele for over 12 years. Always very happy with the Feng Shui readings she does for us yearly, we often refer to and use as guidance throughout each year.

Michele has helped us with the purchase of our homes.

Happily, highly recommended Michele when you need a Feng Shui master for your house, office, and guidance yearly to get you through the year, year after year fan. Michele is very warm, approachable and brings a beautiful energy within her presents. **Aria & Michael Van Uffelen**

Michele Castle is an amazing Fengshui master and has done a very detailed informative book for my home and family. The detailed charts and reports gave us great insight, her amazing experience and explanations help guide us with what the energy is bringing with the year and elements. It has helped us be best prepared, even for the best Feng Shui for our business and money as well.

I am grateful for Michelle's guidance, and I trust her and highly recommend her to my family and friends for her in-depth Feng Shui knowledge. **Bass Tadros**

I have been fortunate enough to have been introduced to Michele and Feng Shui at least 6 years ago. It came about around the trials and tribulations I was having with the building and surroundings I lived and continue to live in. Well, I took on the recommendation to have her check the place out and was pleasantly surprised at her findings and cures and hence allowing peace and harmony to return to my home again. I have completed some courses with Michele and am amazed at how knowledgeable, intuitive, and magical she is... brilliant Feng shui master in my books. I continue to use her for annual assessment of energy flows etc for my home and other aspects of my life.

Love her work and her as a professional being that she is. I highly recommend Michele as a Feng Shui expert and teacher. **Bhavna Mistry**

Since I first met Michele from Complete Feng Shui eight years ago, she has guided me on energetically restoring my house's virtues, found me a landscape artist to design the Garden of Eden of my dreams and sailed me onto the sweet shores of fulfilling romance. She is my go-to Guru and a master of her craft. Monica wood

Michelle is always helpful and willing to advise what works best for everyone in our household. We have engaged her service for over 10 years now on property purchase and annual readings. She is always friendly and so easy to work with. Highly recommend her service. **Frank Walsh**

A must read! Be empowered with these easy tips to enhance your everyday life.

I highly recommend you invest in harnessing the Feng Shui expertise of Michele Vos Castle to live your best, abundant life and maximise your positive energy to sustain a happy life and an overall sense of well-being.

Margie Bryant - Life By Design

Quiet simply I am amazed. I have done some research on the art of feng shui.

This book was incredibly knowledgeable, practical, very easy to read, and it appears Michele knows her stuff 10/10 **J T Jewel**

My life has positively transformed itself after reading, adjusting and following Michele's knowledge. I am so deeply grateful and will be recommending this gem of a book to my clients. **Odette Linton**

www.ingramcontent.com/pod-product-compliance
Lightning Source LLC
Chambersburg PA
CBHW061809290426
44109CB00031B/2972